SAINT JOHN
on
Prayer

Translated by A. M. Casiday

SLG Press
Convent of the Incarnation
Fairacres Parker Street
Oxford OX4 1TB England
www.slgpress.co.uk

Fourth Impression 2019

ISBN 978-0-7283-0166-5
ISSN 0307-1405

Acknowledgement

The 19th century icon, 'Christ and John' *is reproduced on the cover by kind permission of Prälat Alois Haas*

Printed by Joshua Horgan, Oxford.

CONTENTS

Introduction 1

First Conference on Prayer 9
(*Conference 9)*

Second Conference on Prayer 36
(*Conference 10*)

Notes 54

INTRODUCTION

Who was John Cassian?

There are, unfortunately, many details about the life of John Cassian that are lost to us—such as the precise dates of his birth and death (reckoned to be *c*.360–435)—and a few other claims that cannot be settled decisively such as his place of birth (with Dobrujea in Romania and Marseilles as the chief contenders for the honour of claiming him).[1] What is generally agreed is that Cassian, together with Germanus, his travelling-companion and (as it were) spokesman, spent a considerable amount of time in the company of the monks of Lower Egypt in the last decade of the fourth century; it is also widely accepted that Cassian was, if not bilingual in Latin and Greek, then at least certainly proficient in Greek. This unusual experience and linguistic proficiency enabled Cassian to play an important role in the transmission of the culture of Egyptian monasticism into the early medieval west.[2]

One of the reasons why these points are subject to controversy is because scholars have recently reacted against an earlier approach to Cassian, whereby Cassian's writings tended to be taken as authoritative, historical claims about Egyptian monasticism. More will need to be said about that in due course, but for the moment it is as well to say that for centuries Cassian has been valued first and foremost for his two major monastic writings, the *Institutes* and the *Conferences*; the works here translated are taken from the first section (out of three) of Cassian's *Conferences*. In the *Institutes*, Cassian set out his programme for monastic renewal in Gaul so as to bring local customs in line with the practices of the pre-eminent monks, the Fathers of the Egyptian Desert. In the *Conferences*, Cassian directed his attention chiefly to the inner significance of those practices and in that way came to dedicate much of his energy to describing the theology of the desert saints.

As western Christians were increasingly cut off from Egypt, Cassian's books filled the gap. An anecdote from the *Life of Fulgentius of Ruspe* makes this clear: Eulalius, Bishop of Syracuse, encouraged Fulgentius (468-533) to read the *Conferences* when he announced to Eulalius his intention of going on a pilgrimage to Egypt; the *Conferences* were actually much sounder, according to the bishop, because the Egyptians were now non-Chalcedonian heretics![3] Clearly, Cassian's works within a few decades of his death had already attained to a level of recognition that would undoubtedly have gratified him, even if in some instances this meant he was sharply criticised.[4] It seems highly probable that, in his time and for generations thereafter, Cassian was regarded as the foremost Latin interpreter of the Desert Fathers.

Cassian's tradition

Here it needs to be said that, contrary to the perspective of some critics,[5] Cassian never claimed to present a 'history' of monasticism, nor indeed did he offer a dispassionate account of the fathers of the Egyptian desert. Rather, Cassian's avowed purpose was to modify the rules and instructions of the Egyptian and Palestinian monks for the benefit of his readers in Gaul.[6] In other words, Cassian's presentation is anything but disinterested. For example, in *Conference* 10, Cassian is keen to denounce any concept of God that is anthropomorphic. His vivid description of the plight of Abba Serapion is justly famous, but it must not escape our notice that Cassian is not observing any of the proprieties that one might expect of a modern historiographer; specifically, he completely omits to mention that the view which he is championing and which Archbishop Theophilus propounded in his festal letter suffered a devastating blow when Theophilus subsequently rounded on the so-called 'intellectuals' (like Cassian, Abba Isaac and the otherwise unknown Deacon Photinus) and drove most of them out of Egypt.[7] Cassian has come in for criticism for failing to mention that historically significant sequel to the event. But such criticism flies wide of the mark, because Cassian's goal is not to relate a sequence of events; it is not even to report the very words of the abbas.[8] Cassian's writings are accordingly partisan and fully engaged. By them, he aims to foster a particular mindset and, sometimes, to eliminate competing views.

It is not insignificant that one of Cassian's favoured words is *traditio* ('tradition'), including its verbal forms, since Cassian's primary goal is to 'tradition', that is, to hand down, the teachings and instructions from Egypt in a way that is topical and appropriate some three decades later. For precisely this reason, it is important for modern readers with a special concern for the history of Egyptian monasticism to be critical in their reading of Cassian; but then, that is always good practice. If we are respectful of Cassian's intentions, we will be less likely to fault him for failing to deliver an 'unedited' account (which, at the risk of being repetitive, he never promised to do in any case) and more receptive to the works as a vehicle for propagating a view of monasticism—and indeed of Christianity—that stands in continuity with the message of the school of thought that is broadly represented amongst the abbas of the Egyptian desert.[9] For our purposes, two of the abbas are particularly important, albeit for different reasons: Isaac and Evagrius.

Abba Isaac and Abba Evagrius

Abba Isaac is the main speaker in both of the conferences here translated. Unlike some of Cassian's interlocutors, Isaac is otherwise known to us as the 'priest of Kellia' (or, 'the Cells').[10] Even though the two conferences that are translated below are far and away the longest reports of Isaac's teaching, it is probable that their account is accurate in its essentials. We are able to conclude this on the strength of other ancient testimonies that situate Isaac within a network of articulate monks who promoted a spiritual interpretation of Scripture the roots of which even in Cassian's day were already sunk deep in Egyptian history.[11] Isaac was the disciple of Cronius (who was himself reportedly a disciple of Anthony the Great) and his successor as priest at Kellia; he is cited a dozen times in the alphabetic collection of the *Sayings of the Desert Fathers*; he was renowned for his learning and his hospitality; but, like many others, he was eventually driven from Egypt in his old age by Theophilus. All of these indications point to Isaac's connections with those abbas whose spiritual pursuits have resulted in their sometimes being characterised as 'intellectuals' or 'allegorists' (which is evidently an even worse thing in the eyes of the critics). Because one of the most prominent Christian proponents of this approach was Origen of Alexandria, Isaac and others of his generation are sometimes referred as 'Origenists'—but this practice is probably best avoided for four reasons. First, Origen for all his greatness was hardly the originator of this approach; certainly Philo of Alexandria had already prepared the way for him. Second, the term appears to originate as a term of abuse applied in a time of controversy, in which respect it can be compared to its counterpart, 'Anthropomorphites': Isaac would no more have called himself an 'Origenist' than Serapion would have called himself an 'Anthropomorphite'. Third, Origen's influence on subsequent generations of Greek Christians was so widespread and variegated that it does not clarify matters at all to use his name in this way. Fourth, much of what is conventionally assumed to have been 'Origenism' cannot be securely dated earlier than the sixth century, when there erupted a second crisis in which Origen's name was unmistakably reduced to a term of abuse.[12] So we do well to forego that unhelpful term.

The second abba who will figure prominently in what follows is Evagrius. Born in Ibora, Pontus (and therefore often called Evagrius of Pontus or, to use the Latin form, *Ponticus*) around 345, Evagrius eventually made his way to the Egyptian desert, c. 382, where he was apprentice to both Macarius the Great and Macarius the Alexandrian. He appears to have died there in 399. According to Palladius, the author of the *Lausiac History,* Evagrius in time had a circle of his own followers. Palladius was himself a member of that circle and was influenced by Evagrius' thinking, even in writing his *Lausiac History.*[13] It is altogether likely that Cassian was also a disciple of Evagrius. This claim, first advanced systematically by the Benedictine scholar Salvatore Marsili, is based upon the literary dependence of some of Cassian's writings upon Evagrius' works.[14] Scholars have adopted Marsili's findings but, in some cases, extended them well beyond the support of solid evidence.[15] In fact, it may be imprudent to make too many assumptions about the nature of Evagrius' influence upon Cassian; certainly, there remains much work to be done on that front. What can be said with confidence, however, is that Evagrius' writings (which are very numerous) frequently provide valuable and illuminating points of comparison with Cassian's writings. Because Evagrius (like Isaac) is connected to several prominent abbas and his teaching is parallel to theirs in a number of instances,[16] it will be convenient for us to look at various pointers to Evagrius' writings for corroboration of the traditional teaching on prayer advanced in these two brief works.

Ceaseless prayer, imageless prayer

Much could be said about the teaching of prayer that is characteristic of this tradition. Abba Isaac's discussions embrace the four generic types of prayer, the place of tears and compunction in praying, an exegesis of the Lord's Prayer, the instability of one's thoughts and how to overcome it in prayer, the usefulness of formulaic prayer, and other topics. But it would perhaps be presumptuous to say much here since the translator's chief aim is that the source material should be read. Even so, it might not be amiss to comment briefly on the great emphasis on unceasing prayer and its practical corollary, imageless prayer.

The teaching on ceaseless prayer expounded in these conferences is motivated not least by a sense that St Paul did not idly enjoin Christians to 'pray without ceasing' (I Thess. 5:17); monks, such as the intrepid Germanus and Cassian, would presumably be in an enviable position to satisfy this requirement, so it is unsurprising to find that verse recurring in their conversations with Isaac. His teaching is simple in essence, if rather more challenging in application: Isaac encourages them to inculcate the habit of constantly responding prayerfully to all circumstances. To promote the successful implementation of this advice, Isaac recommends an all-purpose verse (Ps 69:2: 'O God, come unto my aid; O Lord, hasten to help me'), thereby eliminating the need to cast about for the right response in a given situation. Ultimately, one's conscious mind (and, to judge from scattered references to dreaming in Cassian's writings, even one's subconscious mind) will be altered by this experience: in all things, one will be aware of God and act accordingly. Yet this is not to say that Cassian was promoting self-conscious religiosity; on the contrary, he reports Isaac's citation of an otherwise unknown comment by Anthony the Great: 'It is not a true prayer when the monk knows himself, or the very thing that he prays'. Through observing Isaac's teaching, one is suffused by a radical sense of God's nearness. We can appreciate the extent of the transformation that Isaac's teaching entails from the following passage:

> So it shall be, when our every love, desire, eagerness, effort and thought, all that we live, speak, breathe will be God. And that unity which is now the Father's with the Son and the Son's with the Father will have transfused our perception and mind, that is, so that just as with a sincere and pure and indissoluble love He loves us, we too will be joined to Him by perpetual and inseparable delight, so linked to Him, to be sure, that whatever we breathe, understand, say would be God.

Such are the fruits of ceaseless prayer. But it is worth considering that this goal is unattainable without taking quite seriously Isaac's categorical denunciation of anthropomorphic tendencies in one's prayer. Although Cassian devotes a significant portion of the tenth conference to a pitiless description of Abba Serapion's fall into despair, he does not say much about the theoretical considerations that inform Serapion's pernicious mistake. In point of fact, he also says very little about the underlying principles of Isaac's teaching. What he does say, however, by way of reporting Photinus' teaching, makes it quite clear why Serapion was mistaken: 'nothing of the sort could befall that infinite, incomprehensible and invisible majesty with the result that it could be encompassed in a human shape and likeness (since that which is by nature incorporeal, uncompounded and simple cannot be conceived by the mind any more than it can be detected by the eyes)'. The adjectives piled on here, 'incorporeal', 'uncompounded' and 'simple', all refer to the divine nature, rather than to one of the persons of the Trinity—a point that is reinforced by Cassian's use of terms like 'Godhead' (Latin: *numen*) in this passage.

By aligning himself with this criticism of anthropomorphism, Cassian is strictly criticising a mistake about conceiving of the divine nature; he is in no sense commenting upon the divine persons. Consequently, Christ is not being discussed here and therefore meditating upon Christ is not precluded by Cassian's position. Maintaining a proper distinction between the nature of God and the divine persons enables Cassian to criticise Serapion and simultaneously to talk about Christ in an orthodox manner as a divine person 'encompassed in a human shape and likeness'. By contrast, since Serapion has formed a habit of envisaging a figure of the Godhead to hold on to whilst praying, he has a fundamentally bankrupt view of what God is and therefore he has eliminated the possibility of understanding God in an orthodox way. Because Cassian's teaching depends upon a close integration of right belief and sound practice, an error as basic as Serapion's (regardless of how understandable it might be) is simply unacceptable.

Cassian does not articulate his position further, but it is certainly consistent with what we have here to suppose that the insurmountable problem with Serapion's ill-considered piety is precisely that it encourages thinking of the divine nature as being corporeal and therefore compounded of elements. In other words, Serapion's style of devotion substitutes a *thing* and addresses prayer to that *thing* in the place of God. By failing in this way to engage with God in prayer, it removes the possibility of cultivating a relationship with God that permeates the whole of one's being along the lines described earlier. It is only through rejecting any images of the Godhead (that is, only through *imageless* prayer) that we can by prayer be so joined to God that everything we do would be God.[17]

Other translations

These two conferences have been translated into English several times. The earliest modern translation is Edgar Gibson's in volume 11 of the Nicene and Post-Nicene Fathers, second series (Oxford: Parker, 1894; subsequently reprinted by T & T Clark of Edinburgh and Wm. Eerdmans of Grand Rapids, MI). Owen Chadwick included these conferences, with a few others, in *Western Asceticism*, a volume of texts in translation that he edited for the Library of Christian Classics (London: SCM, 1958). Similarly, Colm Luibhéid presented these two conferences amongst others in his volume *John Cassian: Conferences* for the Classics of Western Spirituality series (New York: Paulist Press, 1985). Most recently, Boniface Ramsey's contribution to the Ancient Christian Writers series, *John Cassian: The Conferences* (New York: Paulist Press, 1997) features these *Conferences* – along with all the other twenty-two conferences (thus making it the first complete English translation). I regret that Luibhéid's translation was not available to me in preparing this one; as for the others, Gibson's and Ramsey's cleave closely to the Latin. Gibson's is such a faithful representation of the Latin that the tortuous structure of Cassian's typically long periods is retained; Ramsey rather sensibly opted to divide some of the lengthiest sentences to make for more intelligible English, and I have done likewise. Ramsey also provides extensive annotation, to which the keen reader is referred. My debt to him in this respect is considerable. Chadwick's translation is probably the best English version available (apart from his decision to include some of Cassian's asides as footnotes and to insert his own footnotes without distinguishing between the two kinds), but its elegance sometimes obscures the underlying Latin and it seems desirable to produce a translation here that will be readable and at the same time a useful support to those who would undertake to read Cassian's Latin (which is eminently worth doing).

Comparable to Chadwick's excellent English translation is the French translation by Eugene Pichery that faces his edition of the Latin text in *Sources chrétiennes* volumes 42, 54 and 64 (Paris: Cerf, 1955-59), though the notes are very sparse. Likewise, Alfons Kemmer has produced a sturdy German translation of extracts from these *Conferences* and others, *Johannes Cassianus. Weisheit der Wüste* (Einsiedlen: Benziger, 1947), though his notes are in no sense comprehensive. For a continental translation that features notes to rival Ramsey's (or indeed Gibson's), we can but be grateful to Mario Degli Innocenti, whose admirable little book *Giovanni Cassiano. Abba, cos'è la preghiera?* (Magnano: Qiqajon, 2000) has proved extremely useful to me.

The critical work of Michael Petschenig in the *Corpus scriptorium ecclesiasticorum latinorum,* volume 13 (Vienna: Gerold, 1866), is the basis of all modern editions of Cassian. Pichery's edition made some improvements, which were taken up in the recent second edition of Petschenig's text (CSEL 13, *editio altera* [Vienna: Verlag der Osterreichischen Akademie der Wissenschaften, 2004]). That edition, which is the work of Gottfried Kreuz, also incorporated numerous references to Evagrius, Basil the Great and other Greek authors. Those references consolidated and advanced upon research into Cassian since Salvatore Marsili's landmark study, *Giovanni Cassiano ed Evagrio Pontico* (Rome: Sant' Anselmo, 1936) and is by that standard alone tremendously valuable. I have based this translation on that text.

THE FIRST CONFERENCE OF ABBA ISAAC

On Prayer

Contents

1. Introduction to the conference
2. Abba Isaac's discourse on what prayer is
3. How pure and sincere prayer can be achieved
4. On the constant movement of the soul, which is compared to a wing or feather
5. On the things that weigh down our mind
6. On the vision that a certain elder saw concerning the listless work of a brother
7. A question: Why is it more difficult to sustain good thoughts than to achieve them?
8. The answer: On the different sorts of prayer
9. On the four kinds of prayer
10. On the established order of the kinds with respect to prayer
11. On supplication
12. On prayer
13. On petition
14. On thanksgiving
15. Whether these four kinds of prayer are necessary simultaneously and all together, or separately and one after the other
16. Toward what kinds of prayer ought we to exert ourselves?
17. That the four types of prayer were instituted by the Lord
18. On the Lord's prayer
19. On its words, 'Your kingdom come'

20. On its words, 'Your will be done'
21. On the supersubstantial, or daily, bread
22. On its words, 'Forgive us our trespasses', etc.
23. On its words, 'Lead us not into temptation'
24 That nothing should be asked other than what is encompassed in the brevity of the Lord's Prayer
25. On an even more sublime kind of prayer
26. On the different causes of compunction
27. On the different kinds of compunction
28. A question: Why is an abundance of tears not within our power?
29. The answer: On the different sorts of compunction which spring from tears
30. That tears ought not be forced when they do not flow spontaneously
31. Abba Anthony's view on the state of prayer
32. On the proof that one has been heard
33. An objection: Confidence in being thus heard only befits the saints
34. The answer: On the different causes for being heard
35. On the prayer that is to be offered inside one's room, with the door closed
36. On the value of short and silent prayer

1. WITH THE HELP of the Lord, the conferences of the elder Abba Isaac that we are now presenting will fulfil what was promised in the second book of the *Institutes* concerning unbroken continuity in prayer.[18] After these things have been unfolded, I think that I shall have satisfied both the commands of Father Castor of blessed memory and your wishes, blessed Father Leontius[19] and holy Brother Helladius –at least, once the length of the book has been excused. For it has been dragged out to a greater length than we intended, despite our efforts not only to restrict what had to be told to a brief account, but even to pass over many things in silence.

So, after he had launched into a long discussion of various precepts (which we have preferred to curtail out of a desire for brevity), at length the blessed Isaac spoke these words:

2. **ISAAC**: (1) 'The whole purpose of the monk and perfection of his heart tends toward continual and uninterrupted perseverance in prayer. So far as it is allowed to human frailty, the monk struggles for a stable tranquillity and perpetual purity of mind, for the sake of which we tirelessly strive in bodily labours no less than we constantly exert ourselves for spiritual contrition.[20] Indeed, between these two there is a kind of reciprocal and inseparable union. For just as the structure of all the virtues tends towards perfection in prayer, so, too, the whole can in no way remain firm and strong unless it has been bound and fitted together with pure prayer as the capstone. (2) So, then, without them the perpetual and constant tranquillity in prayer about which we are speaking cannot be attained or perfected; and, to the same extent, the very same virtues which support it cannot be completed without assiduously pursuing it.

'So, then, we can neither treat rightly of prayer's effect, nor with a hasty discourse plunge into its final purpose (which is attained through effort in all the virtues), without first having enumerated and discussed one by one all the things that must be either cut out or else prepared in order to attain it. Thus, in keeping with the teaching of the Gospel parable, such things as pertain to the building of that spiritual and most high tower will have been tallied up and diligently considered in advance [cf. Luke 13:28]. (3) But even once these things have been prepared in advance, they will be useless and will not bear the lofty peak of perfection to be put upon them—unless first all the waste of the vices is cleared away and the ruin and debris of the passions is dug out. Then can the foundations of simplicity and humility be put down most firmly on the (so to speak) living and solid soil of our heart, or rather on that gospel rock [cf. Luke 6:48]. After being built by these efforts, the tower of spiritual virtues can be stood fast, and raised to the furthest heights of heaven in the confidence of its stability. (4) And once it rests upon such foundations, even when the massive storms of passions break over it; even when the violent surges of persecutions pound it like a battering ram; yes, even when a savage tempest of adversarial spirits slams into it and attacks it—even then, not only will no ruin overtake it, but the attack itself will not disturb it in the slightest.

3. (1) 'So, then, that prayer may be made with due fervour and purity, the following points must be observed in their entirety.

'First, all care for fleshly things must be altogether excised. Next, even the very memory of enterprises and projects—much less care for them—must not be entertained in the slightest.[21] Likewise, gossip, idle talk or chatter, and clowning must be cut off. The disturbance of anger above all and sadness must be entirely destroyed. And the poisonous shoot of fleshly lust and love of money must be pulled up by the roots. (2) Once these vices, and others like them which are also apparent to the eyes of men, have been entirely removed and excised, and that cleansing and purification such as we said is accomplished by pure simplicity and innocence has occurred, then the first thing is that unshakeable foundations of deep humility must be laid. These foundations are strong enough to support a tower that will be built up into the skies. Next, the spiritual infrastructure of virtues needs to be put down on those foundations. The soul must be restrained from all wandering and slippery digressions, so that by degrees it may begin to ascend to the contemplation of God and to the understanding of spiritual matters.[22] (3) For it is sure that whatever our mind has been entertaining before the time for prayer will occur to us when we pray as our memory brings it up.

'For this reason, we need to prepare ourselves before the time for prayer to be as we would wish to be found when we pray, since the mind is shaped in its petitions by its previous state. As we bend ourselves to pray, images of the same deeds or words or thoughts in keeping with our previous condition will dance before our eyes to anger us, or sadden us, or recall our former projects and lusts, or shake us with stupid laughter—it is shameful even to say it!—by amusing us with some silly word or deed, or turn us back to our former wandering ways. (4) And so we must take care before prayer to exclude from the shrine of our heart whatever we do not want to rush in while we are praying. In this way, we can fulfil the words of the Apostle: "Pray without ceasing" [I Thess. 5:17], and "In every place, raising holy hands without wrath or argument" [I Tim. 2:8]. In any case, we will not be able to satisfy that command unless our mind has been purified from every stain of the vices and dedicated to the virtues as to its natural good, so that it pastures constantly on contemplating Almighty God.

4. (1) 'The soul's character is, after all, not ineptly compared to an exceedingly fine feather or a very light wing.[23] If it has not been damaged by having been soaked to its harm by any moisture from without, it is as it were borne up to the heavenly heights with the aid of the slightest breath, owing to how distinctly mobile it is. Yet if it has been weighted by the sprinkling and soaking of any moisture, it will in no way be carried into heavenly flights, winged by its natural mobility; instead, it will be dragged down to the depths of the earth by the heavy moisture it has taken on. (2) So, too, our mind. If it has not been weighted down by the vices that touch it and by worldly cares, or harmed by the moisture of poisonous lust, it will be carried off to the heights as it were by the natural blessing of its purity, elevated by the lightest breath of spiritual meditation. Taking its leave of lowly and earthly things, it is borne across to things heavenly and invisible. It is therefore fitting that we are well warned by these precepts from Our Lord: "See to it that your hearts are not weighed down in drinking and drunkenness and earthly cares" [Luke 21:34]. (3) Thus, if we want our prayers to penetrate not only the heavens, but even what is beyond the heavens, let us have a care for our soul. Let us lead it back to its natural fineness, purged from all earthly vices and cleansed from all the stains of the passions. In this way, the soul's prayer may ascend to God, unhindered by the weight of any vices.

5. (1) 'Let us note the ways in which the Lord points out that the soul is weighed down. He did not put down adultery, fornications, murder, blasphemies, or rapes, which everyone knows are deadly and damnable, but rather drinking, drunkenness, and the cares or anxieties of this world. No worldly man avoids these things or considers them damnable. Indeed, even some who call themselves monks—it is shameful even to say it!—entangle themselves in these very same

distractions as though they were harmless or even useful. (2) These three things can literally weigh down the soul, thus separating it from God and bringing it down to earthly matters, it is nevertheless quite easy for us to avoid them, since we are so far removed from all interaction with this world and in any case never have anything to do with these visible cares and drunkenness and drinking.

'But there is another kind of drinking that is no less dangerous, a spiritual drunkenness that is harder to avoid, and a care and anxiety for this world that often entraps us—and this even after we have completely renounced all of our goods, even as we abstain from wine and all feasting; even when we live in solitude! It is of them that the prophet says: "Awake, you who are drunk but not with wine" [cf. Joel 1:5 LXX]. (3) Another says, "Be stupefied and amazed and stagger, be drunk but not with wine" [Isa. 29:9]. Consequently, the wine of this drunkenness must necessarily be the "fury of the dragons" according to the prophet [Deut. 32:33 LXX], and hear now from what root that same wine comes: "From the vineyard of Sodom is their vine and their branches from Gomorra" [Deut. 32:32 LXX]. (4) Would you like to know more about the fruit of that vine and the seed of that branch? "Their grape is the grape of gall, their cluster is of bitterness" [ibid]. If we are not purged from all vices and sober from the drink of all passions, even apart from the drunkenness of wine and the excess of all that feasting, our heart will be weighed down by an even more poisonous drunkenness and drinking.

'The fact that worldly cares can sometimes befall even us who consort with none of the deeds of this world is clearly shown according to the rule of the Elders. They have decreed that whatever goes beyond the necessities of daily food, and the unavoidable needs of the flesh, is evidence for worldly cares and anxieties. (5) This happens, for example, if we want to protract a job by longer toil and work in order to gain for ourselves two or three *solidi*, when earning just one *solidus* would satisfy the needs of our body; or else when we arrange it so that we become owners of three or four tunics, although a covering of two tunics would suffice for use by night and by day; or else when, out of delight in worldly ambition and comfort, we build four or five cells—and these richly appointed and larger than need requires—although a dwelling of one or two cells would suffice: in such a way, we prefer the passion of worldly lusts whenever we can.

6. (1) 'Surest proofs teach us that this does not come to pass without the prompting of demons. Once a highly accomplished elder was passing by the cell of a certain brother who was suffering from this spiritual disease which we have described and was at that moment restlessly exerting himself in his daily practices of building and repairing what was unnecessary. And from a distance the elder watched him trying to break a very hard stone with a heavy hammer, and saw a certain Ethiopian[24] standing over him and striking the blows of the hammer together with him with joined and clasped hands, and stirring him to diligence in that work with fiery encouragement. The elder stood there for quite some time, astounded by the influence of that most fierce demon and the deception of such an illusion. (2) Even when the brother was worn out with exhaustion and wanted to rest and make an end of the work, he would catch another wind at that spirit's stirring and was driven to take up his hammer again and not to desist from devoting himself to the task that he had undertaken. Being in this way indefatigably sustained by the demon's incitements, the brother did not perceive the injury that so great labour was doing him.

'At length the elder, deeply troubled by the demon playing such a terrible game, turned aside to the brother's cell. After greeting him, the elder asked, "What is this work, brother, which you are doing?" And the brother said, "We are working at this terribly hard stone, and we are hardly able to break it at all." (3) To this the elder replied, "You were right to say 'we'! For you were not alone when you were striking it; rather, there was with you another whom you did not see, who was standing by you—not so much as a helper in the task, but as a ruthless taskmaster."

'And so, merely abstaining from those affairs which we cannot accomplish even if we wanted to undertake or complete them, or despising those matters which, if we pursued them, would make us stand out in the front rank among spiritual persons as well as among worldly men, will not prove that the disease of worldly vanity is not present in our minds. It will only be proved when with unbending mental rigour we reject those things that lie in our power and that seem veiled with a kind of honesty. These things may seem trivial and unimportant, and we may find that they are permitted as matters of indifference by those who belong to our calling. (4) But in fact by their character they weigh down the mind no less than those more important things which typically intoxicate the senses of worldly people—as befits their status—and which do not allow the monk to lay aside earthly filth and aspire to God, on whom his attention should always be fixed. In the monk's case, even a tiny separation from the highest good must be considered immediate death and most ruinous destruction.

(5) 'And when the mind has been established in such a peaceful condition, or rather has been freed from the snares of all fleshly passions, and the heart adheres with its most tenacious fixity to the only true and highest good, then will the monk fulfil the Apostolic precept: "Pray without ceasing"; and: "in every

place lifting up holy hands without wrath and disputing" [I Thess. 5:17, I Tim. 2:8]. For when the mind's thoughts are, so to speak, engrossed by this purity (if we can say so) and are re-fashioned from their fallen earthly state into a spiritual and angelic likeness, then whatever it accepts, whatever it attempts, whatever it does, will be perfectly pure and sincere prayer.' [25]

7. **GERMANUS**: (1) 'Would that we could perpetually keep those spiritual thoughts in like manner and with the same ease with which we usually conceive the seeds of them! Yet once they have been conceived in our hearts, either through the remembrance of Scriptures or the recollection of some spiritual actions or indeed the consideration of heavenly mysteries, all too quickly they vanish, flying as it were unseen. (2) And when our mind has found some other occasions for spiritual perceptions,[26] different perceptions slip in again and those that had been grasped are scattered with slippery speed; thus, because the soul cannot of its own power keep steadfast, nor have any stability with respect to holy thoughts, it must be believed that the soul conceived them by chance and not by effort, even when it somehow seems to keep them. After all, how can it be thought that their rising should be ascribed to our will, when to persevere with them is not in our power?

(3) 'But so as not to digress any further from the discussion that had begun through considering this question, and delay any longer the explanation of the nature of prayer that was being advanced, let us set this subject aside for its own time; at this precise moment, what we ask to be informed about is the character of prayer, particularly since the blessed Apostle exhorts us to cease from it at no time, when he says, "Pray without ceasing" [I Thess. 5:17]. (4) So, first, we want to be informed about its character—i.e., *which* prayer ought to be offered up always—and, second, how we can obtain this

(whatever it is) and practise it without ceasing. We are shown by Your Holiness's discourse in which you defined the aim of the monk and the peak of all perfection as consisting in the perfection of prayer, and by daily experience, that it cannot be accomplished by a paltry intention of the heart.'

8. **ISAAC**: (1): 'I take it that all the types of prayers cannot be grasped without tremendous purity of heart and soul and the illumination of the Holy Spirit, for there are as many conditions and characters as can be produced in one soul, or rather in all souls. (2) Even though we know that we cannot see all kinds of prayers owing to our dullness of heart, we will try nevertheless to relate them in some order, insofar as the poverty of our experience enables us to understand them. The very prayers themselves will be altered moment by moment according to the degree of purity to which each mind attains and according to the character of the state to which it is either being inclined—owing to what happens to it—or in which it is being renewed by its own efforts; it is therefore most certain that nobody can always offer up uniform prayers. (3) For a person prays in one way when he is excited, in another way when oppressed by the weight of sadness or despair; in another when invigorated by spiritual accomplishments, in another when cast down by a mass of assaults; in another when asking pardon for his sins, in another when asking to obtain grace or some virtue or else praying for the annihilation of some sin; in another when pricked by the thought of Gehenna and fear of future judgment, in another when radiant with the hope and desire of good things to come; in another when he is in exigencies and dangers, in another when he is in peace and security; in another when he is illuminated by revelations of heavenly mysteries, and in another when he is constrained by barrenness in virtues and dryness in perceptions.

9. (1) 'But even once these things concerning the character of prayer have been enumerated (even if not so fully as the importance of the subject cries out for, but as fully as the lack of time permits—and certainly as fully as our meagre wit and dull heart are up to undertaking!) a greater difficulty now awaits us in expounding one by one the different kinds of prayer which the Apostle distinguished in his four-fold account, when he says, "I exhort therefore first of all that supplications, prayers, intercessions, thanksgivings be made" [I Tim 2:1]. It cannot be doubted in the slightest that this division was not made idly by the Apostle.

(2) 'The first thing to be investigated is what is meant by supplication, by prayer, by intercession and by thanksgiving. Next it must be asked whether these four kinds are to be attempted all at once by one who prays: that is, are they all to be linked together in each and every prayer? Or are they to be offered one by one in turn (so that, for instance, it is proper that supplications should be made at one time, prayers at another, intercessions at another, and thanksgivings at yet another)? Or indeed ought one person to make supplications to God, another prayers, another intercessions and yet another thanksgivings, in keeping with the measure of maturity to which each mind is advancing by the effort of its intention?

10. 'First, we must treat of the distinctive properties of the names and words, and discuss what the difference between prayer and supplication and intercession is. Second, we must likewise consider whether they are to be produced separately or all together. Third, we must investigate whether the very order itself which is thus set down by the Apostle's authority has anything further to teach the hearer, or whether the distinction simply is to be taken and the fact that they were arranged thus by him is to be regarded as a matter of no importance. Now that

seems to me utterly absurd, for it should not be believed that the Holy Spirit uttered anything through the Apostle casually or without purpose. And so let us treat of them separately, as the Lord grants us, in the same order in which we began.

11. '"I exhort therefore first of all that supplications be made ..." *Supplication* is an imploring, or petition, about sins whereby one who is struck with sorrow for present or past deeds asks for pardon. [27]

12. (1) '*Prayers* are how we offer or vow something to God, which is called *euchê* ("vow") in Greek.[28] Thus, where in Greek we read *tas euchas mou tô Kuriô apodôsô* in Latin we read, "I will pay my vows unto the Lord" [Ps. 115:14], though it could be rendered in keeping with the precise wording as follows: "I will pay my prayers to the Lord". And what we find in Eccles. [5:3 LXX], "If you vow a vow to the Lord, do not delay to pay it," is similarly written in Greek: *ean euxê euchên tô kuriô* (i.e., "If you pray a prayer unto the Lord, do not delay to pay it"). (2) Here is how that will be fulfilled by each of us: We *pray* when, renouncing this world and having died to all activities and the worldly way of life, we pledge to serve the Lord with every intention of our heart. We *pray* when, despising secular honours and scorning earthly gains, we promise to cling to the Lord in all contrition of heart and humility of spirit. We *pray* when we promise always to exhibit the purest chasteness of body and imperturbable patience, or when we vow that the roots of anger or of sorrow that bring about death will be utterly extirpated from our heart. If we ever fail to do these things, being undone by sloth and returning to our old vices, we shall be guilty of our prayers and vows and it will be said of us, "It is better not to vow, than to vow and not to pay it" [Eccles. 5:4 LXX]—or, as it can be said in keeping with the Greek, "It is better not to pray, than to pray and not pay it".

13. '*Intercessions* come in the third place, which we are accustomed to offer up for others too, while we are filled with fervour of spirit, making request either for those who are dear to us or for the peace of the whole world,[29] and we pray "for all men, for kings and all that are in authority", to use the very words of the Apostle [I Tim. 2:1–2].

14. '*Thanksgivings* come in the fourth place, which the mind conveys to God through ineffable outpourings, either when it recalls the past benefits of God or contemplates the present ones, or indeed looks forward to those great ones in the future which God has prepared for those who love Him [cf. I Cor. 2:9]. And sometimes, in this disposition, richer prayers are offered up, while, by gazing with pure eyes on those rewards of the saints which are laid up for the future, our spirit is moved to pour out ineffable thanks to God with tremendous joy.

15. (1) 'From these four kinds of prayer, the occasions for richer entreaties sometimes arise; for we know that most fervent and fiery prayers proceed very frequently from the kind of supplication which is born of compunction for sins, from the state of prayer which flows forth from assurance in our oblations and the fulfilment of our vows in pureness of conscience, from the intercessions that proceed from the warmth of charity and from thanksgiving that is generated from the consideration of God's benefits and his greatness and kindness. Thus it is clear that the aforementioned kinds of prayer are found to be useful and necessary for everybody, and consequently in one and the same person a change of perception results in the utterance of pure and most fervent entreaties, sometimes supplications, sometimes prayers, sometimes intercessions. Even so, the first kind seems more especially pertinent to beginners who are still vexed by the stings and memory of their vices; the second, to those who already have attained some elevation of mind in spiritual progress and

seeking after virtues; the third to those who, having fulfilled their vows by their works, are prompted to intercede for others as well by the consideration of their weakness and the zeal of their own love; the fourth to those who, having already plucked the thorn of guilty conscience from their hearts, are now in safety considering with the purest of minds the bounties and compassions of God that He has either granted in the past or is presently giving or preparing for the future, are in this way carried with most fervent hearts to that fiery prayer which can be neither embraced nor expressed by the human mouth.

(2) 'And yet sometimes the mind which progresses to that true condition of purity and has already begun to be rooted in it, conceiving all these things at one and the same time and flying around all of them like a kind of incomprehensible and most greedy flame, is accustomed to pour out prayers of purest vigour to God—which the Spirit Himself, intervening with unutterable groans that we do not know [cf. Rom. 8:26], sends to God—conceiving at that moment, I say, and ineffably pouring forth in supplications things such as not only cannot proceed from the mouth, but also cannot even be recollected by the mind at another time. (3) And so it happens that in whatever degree someone stands, he is found sometimes to offer up pure and intent prayers. Even at that first and lowly order which is concerned with the recollection of future judgment, one who still remains under the punishment of terror and the fear of scrutiny is so smitten at that time that he is filled with keenness of spirit from the richness of supplication no less than one who, reflecting upon and dwelling on the bounties of God in the purity of his heart, is undone with ineffable joy and delight. He begins to love more who knows that he has been forgiven more, in keeping with the Lord's claim [cf. Luke 7:27].

16. 'However, through advancing in life and perfecting virtues we ought rather to strive for those kinds of prayer which are poured out either from the contemplation of future goods or the warmth of charity or which (to speak more humbly and in keeping with the order of beginners) at least are generated by the acquisition of some virtue or the annihilation of some fault. Otherwise, we will be in no way able to attain to those loftier types of entreaties about which we spoke earlier, if our mind has not been raised, little by little and step by step, through the usual order of those intercessions.

17. (1) 'The Lord Himself deigned to initiate these four types of entreaties for us by His own example, so that even in this He might fulfil what was said of Him, "which Jesus began to do and teach" [Acts 1:11]. For He resorted to the class of supplication when He said, "Father, if it is possible, let this cup pass from me" [Matt. 26:39]; or this which is sung in His person in the Psalm [21:2]: "My God, my God, look upon me; why have You forsaken me?" — and other similar passages. (2) It is a prayer when He says, "I have glorified You upon the earth, I have completed the work that You gave me to do" [John 17:4] and, "For their sakes I sanctify myself, so that they also may be sanctified in truth" [John 17:19]. It is an intercession when He says, "Father, I will that those whom You have given me should themselves be with me where I am, so that they may see my glory which You have given me" [John 17:24]; or in any case when He says, "Father, forgive them for they do not know what they are doing" [Luke 23:34]. (3) It is thanksgiving when He says, "I confess to You, Father, Lord of heaven and earth, because You have hidden these things from the wise and the prudent and have revealed them to little children. Even so, Father, for thus it was pleasing to you" [Matt. 11:25–26], or in any case when He said, "Father, I

thank You because You heard me, though I knew that You always hear me" [John 11:41–42].

'But even though Our Lord made a distinction between these four kinds of prayers as being offered separately and one by one in keeping with the scheme which we embrace, He nevertheless showed by His own deeds that they can all be embraced at one and the same time in a perfect entreaty—particularly in that prayer which we read at the close of St John's Gospel that He poured forth so copiously. (4) From that text (though it is too long to work through the whole thing) the diligent inquirer can learn from the sequence of the passage itself that these things are so. The Apostle, too, in his Epistle to the Philippians [4:6] has clearly expressed the same meaning while putting these four kinds of prayer in a slightly different order, and shown that sometimes they ought to be offered together in the fervour of a single entreaty when he said, "But in every prayer and supplication with thanksgiving, let your requests be known unto God". By this, he wished us to learn especially that in prayer and in supplication thanksgiving should be mixed with intercession.

18. (1) 'And so a state that is still more lofty and exalted follows upon these kinds of entreaties, which is made of the contemplation of God alone and of the warmth of charity; by it the mind, which has been undone by and cast into the love of Him, speaks with God most intimately, as with its own father, in a special devotion. (2) The formula of the Lord's Prayer establishes that we ought diligently to seek after this state, when it says, "Our Father" [Matt. 6:9]. Now when with our own voice we confess that God the Lord of the Universe is our Father, we profess straightway that we have been called forth from a servile condition to the "adoption of sons" [Eph. 1:5]. Then we add, "who are in the heavens", so that we may hasten with greatest eagerness to that place where we acknowledge that our

Father abides, shunning with all horror abiding in the present life that we live on this earth as a pilgrimage, and whatever separates us greatly from our Father; and that we may admit nothing that, by making us unworthy of this profession of ours and the honour of such an adoption, would cheat us of our patrimony as being unfit for it and make us incur the wrath of His justice and severity.

(3) 'Once we have advanced to the order and level of sons, we shall at once be aflame with the devotion appropriate to good sons, so that we shall direct our every desire not to our own uses but to the glory of our Father, saying to Him, "Hallowed be Your name" and thus testifying that our desire, our joy, is our Father's glory as we have become imitators of Him who said, "He who speaks of himself seeks his own glory, but he who seeks the glory of the one who sent him is true and there is no injustice in him" [John 7:18]. After all, the "vessel of election" [Acts 9:15], filled with this desire, chose rather to be anathema from Christ if only it would gain for Him a larger family and the salvation of the whole people of Israel would redound to the glory of his Father [cf. Rom. 9:3, I Cor. 9:20]. (4) As one who knew that no one can die for life, he was safe in choosing to perish for Christ. Again, he says, "We rejoice when we are weak but you are strong" [II Cor. 13:9].

'And what wonder if the "vessel of election" chose to be anathema from Christ for the sake of Christ's glory and the conversion of his brethren and the benefit of the heathen, when Micah the prophet willed that he might be a liar and a stranger to the inspiration of the Holy Spirit if only the people of the Jewish nation might escape the plagues and the exile into captivity which he had foretold in his proclamation; he said, "Would that I were not a man who has the Spirit and that instead I spoke a lie" [Mic. 2:11]. And this is to pass over the

Lawgiver's desire, who did not refuse to perish with his kinsfolk even when they were going to die; he said, "I beseech You, Lord—this people have sinned a great sin, but either forgive them this offence or, if not, blot me out of Your book which You have written" [Exod. 32:31–32].

(5) 'But when it is said, "Hallowed be Your name," it may quite satisfactorily be taken in this manner: "God's hallowing is our perfection". So when we say to Him, "Hallowed be Your name," this is what we are saying in other words: "Make us such, Father, that we may be able to understand and grasp what Your hallowing is, or at least that You may appear holy in our spiritual way of life. Now this is effectively fulfilled in us, when people see our good works and glorify our Father who is in the heavens [cf. Matt. 5:16].

19. 'The pure mind's second petition wishes for the kingdom of its Father to come straightway. This means either that situation whereby Christ reigns daily in the saints which happens when, once the devil's rule has been expelled from our hearts by the destruction of foul vices, God begins to rule over us by the sweet smell of virtues [cf. II Cor. 2:14] and charity reigns in our hearts when fornication has been overcome; tranquillity, when rage is conquered; and humility, when pride is trodden under foot; or else it means that which is promised in due course to all the perfect and the sons of God, when it will be said to them by Christ: "Come, you who are blessed of My Father, receive the kingdom prepared for you from the foundation of the world" [Matt. 25:34]—whilst the mind, with fixed and steady purpose, as it were, desires and looks for Him and says, "Your kingdom come". For it knows by the testimony of its own conscience that, when He shall appear, it will immediately be His partner. No guilty person would dare to say or to wish for this, since nobody would want to face the tribunal of the Judge,

who knew that at His coming he would receive at once not a prize or reward for his merits but a punishment.

20. (1) 'The third is the petition of sons: "Your will be done on earth just as in heaven". There can be no greater prayer now than to wish that earthly things should be made equal with heavenly things. And what else is it to say "Your will be done on earth just as in heaven," than that men may be like angels and that just as God's will is fulfilled by the latter in heaven, likewise those on earth may do not their own but His will? [30] The only person who could say this with earnest desire is one who believes that God disposes everything that is seen—whether good or ill—for our benefit and that He is more careful and solicitous for our salvation and needs than we are for our own selves. (2) Or in any case it may be taken thus: God's will is the salvation of all, according to this statement by the blessed Paul: "... who wills everyone to be saved and to come to knowledge of the truth" [I Tim. 2:4]. About this will, the prophet Isaiah also says in the person of God the Father, "And all My will shall be done" [Isa. 46:10]. So when we say to Him, "Your will be done on earth just as in heaven," we pray in other words for this: that all those who dwell on earth may be saved, just like those who are in heaven, O Father, by the knowledge of You.

21. (1) 'Next: "Give us this day our *epiousion*—i.e., 'supersubstantial'—bread", which another Evangelist calls "daily bread" [Luke 11:3]. The former designates the quality of its noble substance, by which it is above all substances (the loftiness of its magnificent holiness exceeds all creatures), whereas the latter expresses the distinctive character of its use and value. When it says "daily", it shows that without it we are unable to live a spiritual life for a single day. (2) When it says "today", it shows that it must be consumed daily and that yesterday's supply of it is insufficient, unless it has also been

given to us today in the same way. Our daily need of it indicates that at all times we ought to pour forth this prayer, since there is no day when we have no need to strengthen our inner man's heart by eating and receiving it. However, when "today" is said, it may be understood with reference to this present life: i.e., "While we are living in this world, provide us with this bread. For we know that it will be given by You to those who deserve it in the future, but we ask that You would lavish it upon us today, since no one will be a partaker of it in that life unless in this life he has been vouchsafed to receive it."

22. (1) '"And forgive us our debts as we also forgive our debtors." O the ineffable mercy of God! Not only has it passed down to us a form of prayer, instituted for us a system of life acceptable to Him, and eradicated both anger and sorrow by the requirements of the traditional form in which He taught us ever to pray; it even gives an opportunity to those who pray and opens a way to them by which they may appeal for God's judgment to be pronounced over them, merciful and kind. In a way, it gives us a power by which we can moderate our Judge's sentence, inducing Him to forgive our offences by the example of our forgiveness when we say to Him, "Forgive us as we also forgive."

(2) 'And so, safely confident in this prayer, one may beseech pardon for one's own offences, if one has dismissed one's own debtors—but *not* the Lord's debtors. For some of us are in the very bad habit of appearing calm and most merciful in respect of those things which are done to God's detriment, however great the crimes may be, but of being found to be harsh and inexorable exactors of debts to ourselves in the case of even the tiniest offences. (3) Now anyone who does not wholeheartedly forgive the brother who has offended him, calls down upon himself by this plea, not forgiveness, but condemnation: by his own

profession, he asks that he himself may be judged more harshly when he says: "Forgive me as I also have forgiven". If he is recompensed according to his own request, what will follow other than that, in keeping with his own example, he will be punished with implacable wrath and a sentence that cannot be appealed against. If therefore we want to be judged mercifully, it behoves us to be merciful ourselves towards those who have trespassed against us. For it will be remitted to us only to the extent that we have remitted to those who have injured us, regardless of how spitefully.

(4) 'There are some who, out of fear, pass over this phrase in silence when this prayer is chanted in church by all the people, lest by professing it they are seen to make themselves liable rather than excuse themselves. What they do not understand is that it is vanity to try offering up these sophistries to the Judge of all, who has chosen to show us in advance how He is going to judge those who beseech Him. As He does not want to be found to be harsh and inexorable in dealing with them, He has outlined the criteria for His judgement, with the result that we should judge our brethren (if they have trespassed against us in anything) in the same manner as we desire to be judged by Him, since there is "judgment without mercy for one who has not shown mercy" [Jas 1:12].

23. (1) 'Next follows, "And lead us not into temptation"—and concerning this there arises a not insignificant question: If we pray that we may not be permitted to be tempted, how will our staying power be proved? Consider the claim, "Everyone who is not tempted, is not proved" [Sir. 34:11]; and again, "Blessed is the man that endures temptation" [Jas 1:12]. So "Lead us not into temptation" does not signify this: "do not allow us ever to be tempted", but rather this: "do not allow us to be overcome when we fall into temptation". (2) Job was tempted,

but was not *led into temptation*, for he did not ascribe foolishness to God, nor did he blasphemously enter into that wilfulness of the Tempter toward which he was drawn [cf. Job 42:7,8; 2:9–10]. Abraham was tempted, Joseph was tempted, but neither of them was *led into temptation*, since neither of them offered his consent to the tempter [cf. Gen. 22:1–8; 39:7–13].

Next follows, "But deliver us from evil"—i.e., do not allow us to be tempted by the devil beyond our ability, but "make with the temptation a way also of escape that we may be able to bear it" [Matt. 6:13].

24. 'Now you see of what sort the method is, and what is the form of prayer which is set for us by the very Judge who is to be prayed to by it. There is contained in it no petition for riches, no consideration of honours, no request for power and strength, no mention of physical health and of temporal life. For the Fashioner of Eternity would have us ask Him for nothing perishable, nothing lowly, nothing time-bound. Therefore anyone who prefers to ask him for something transitory and perishable, whilst foregoing these eternal requests, will offer the greatest insult to His majesty and bounty—and by the lowliness of the prayer will also incur the Judge's indignation rather than His propitiation.

25. 'So then this prayer seems to contain all the fullness of perfection in that it was instituted and established by the Lord's own authority; and yet it leads His familiars through a loftier grade to that fiery prayer which is known or experienced by very few, but (that I may speak more precisely) is ineffable. I do not say that this prayer, which transcends all human understanding, is not distinguished by any sound of the voice or movement of the tongue or pronunciation of words. Rather it is this prayer that the mind, enlightened by the infusion of that heavenly light,

does not describe by restricted, human eloquence; but, with its senses gathered together, it abundantly gives forth as it were from some most plentiful fountain and ineffably talks to God. In that most fleeting moment of time, it produces so many things that the mind, once it turns back upon itself, is incapable of speaking readily about them, either eloquently or summarily. Our Lord also similarly anticipated this condition by the form of those entreaties which He is said to have poured forth silently when He withdrew alone into the mountain; when set in an agony of prayer He even shed drops of blood in an inimitable example of purpose.

26. (1) 'But regardless of the experience with which one is endowed, who is able to expound sufficiently the varieties and very reasons and grounds of being struck with sorrow, by which the mind, inflamed and set on fire, is incited to pure and most fervent prayers? By way of example, we will propose a few of them, as much as we can recollect by the Lord's illumination. Sometimes when we sing a verse from a given Psalm, this provides us with an occasion for fiery prayer. Meanwhile, the harmonious melody of a brother's voice excites torpid souls to intense entreaty. (2) We know, too, that the cantor's ornamentation and dignity greatly contribute to the fervour of those present. No less than that, a perfect person's exhortation and spiritual conversation[31] has often raised the sentiments of those nearby to exceedingly rich prayer. We also know that we have been no less moved to profound compunction by the death of a brother or someone dear to us. The remembrance of our indifference and negligence has sometimes also aroused a saving fervour of spirit in us. And so no one can doubt that in this way there are not lacking innumerable opportunities by which the indifference and sleepiness of our minds can be stirred to action through God's grace.

27. 'But it is no less difficult to track how, and in what way, the very moments of compunction themselves are produced from the spirit's innermost recesses. Frequently, in the spirit's ineffable joy and keenness, the fruit of saving compunction emerges in such a way that it breaks forth into shouts because of the greatness of its uncontrollable joy, and the heart's liveliness and greatness of exultation penetrates even into a neighbour's cell. But sometimes the mind is hidden in such silence within the secrets of profound stillness that the astonishment of sudden illumination completely restrains all sound of the voice and the stunned spirit either keeps all its feelings inside or parts with them and pours forth its desires to God in "groans that cannot be uttered" [Rom. 8:26]. And on still other occasions, it is filled to overflowing with compunction and grief so that it cannot express them except in a flood of tears.'

28. **GERMANUS**: (1) 'For my part, insignificant as it is, I am not ignorant of this feeling of being stricken with sorrow. Often, when tears well up at the recollection of my faults, at the Lord's visitation I have been so invigorated by the ineffable joy which you described that the greatness of the joy has reminded me not to despair of their forgiveness. I suppose there is nothing loftier than that state, if only its renewal could be brought about by our will. (2) Sometimes, when with all my strength I wish to stir myself up to a similar tearful state of sorrow and put all my errors and sins before my eyes, I am not able to bring back that rich weeping: my eyes remain like some really hard flint, so that not a single tear falls from them. Therefore to the same extent that I rejoice in that profusion of tears, I sorrow that I cannot recover it at will.'

29. **ISAAC**: (1) 'Not every profusion of tears is drawn forth by one feeling or one power. For in one way that weeping emerges from our heart when it has been pricked with sorrow by the

spines of sins (about which it is said: "I have laboured in my groaning, every night will I wash my bed; I will water my couch with my tears", and "Day and night let tears run down like a torrent; give yourself no rest, nor let the pupil of your eye be still"; [Ps. 6:6–7; Lam. 2:18]). (2) And in another way emerges the weeping that arises from contemplation of the eternal goods and desire for that future glory, for the sake of which even richer springs of tears burst forth from unbearable joy and unbounded keenness, whilst our soul thirsts for the mighty living God, saying, "When shall I come and appear in the sight of God? For me, tears have been my bread day and night" [Ps. 41:3–4] and proclaiming with daily crying and lamentation, "Woe is me that my sojourning has been prolonged" and "My soul has been a sojourner for too long" [Ps. 119:5–6].

(3) 'In another way flow the tears which, quite apart from any awareness of deadly sins, proceed all the same from the fear of hell and the remembrance of that terrible judgment, with the terror that struck the prophet who prayed to God, saying: "Do not enter into judgment with Your servant, for in Your sight no one living shall be justified" [Ps. 142:2][32]. And there is another kind of tears which are engendered, not by one's own conscience, but by the recalcitrance and sins of others: it was with this kind of tears that Samuel is described as having wept for Saul [cf. I Kings 15:35], and both the Lord in the Gospel [Luke 19:41ff.] and Jeremiah in earlier times for the city of Jerusalem, saying, "Who will give me water for a head and a fountain of tears for my eyes, and I shall weep both day and night for the slain of the daughter of my people" [Jer. 9:1].

(4) 'And indeed such were those tears, concerning which we hear in Psalm 101:[10], "I have eaten ashes for my bread, and mingled my cup with weeping". Certainly, they were not caused by the same feeling as those which emerge from the person of

the penitent in Psalm 6, but are due to the anxieties of this life and its difficulties and tribulations by which the righteous living in this world are oppressed. The text of the psalm itself is not the only thing that clearly shows this: it is done even by the psalm's title, which, in the person of that poor person about whom it is said in the Gospel, "blessed are the poor in spirit, for theirs is the kingdom of heaven" [Matt. 5:3], is described as "the prayer of a poor person, when he was distressed and poured forth his petition to God" [Ps.101:1].

30. (1) 'Very different from these tears are those which are squeezed out of dry eyes when the heart is hard. Although we cannot believe that they are utterly fruitless (after all, the attempt to shed them is made from good intent, particularly by those who have as yet been unable to arrive at perfect knowledge or to be thoroughly cleansed from the stain of past or present vices) nonetheless this flow of tears should not be forced out in this way by those who have already advanced in the disposition of virtue. Nor should the weeping of the "outward man" be attempted with great labour—even if the weeping is produced somehow, it will never be able to attain the richness of spontaneous tears. (2) Instead, drawing down the soul of the suppliant by his endeavours, these tears will humiliate the suppliant, submerge him in human affairs and remove the stunned mind of one who prays from the celestial heights where it ought to be unwaveringly fixed, and it will compel the mind to languish from sterile and forced teardrops, once the purpose of its prayers has been relaxed.

31. 'For you to perceive the disposition of true prayer, I offer, not my own judgment, but the blessed Anthony's. We have known him sometimes so to have persisted in prayer that, his mind being in a transport of prayer, when the sun began to appear we have heard him proclaim in the fervour of his spirit,

"Why, O sun, do you impede me, who have been praying until now, so as to draw me from the glory of that true light?" And this heavenly and superhuman view of the end of prayer is also his: "It is not a true prayer when the monk knows himself, or the very thing that he prays".

'For our part, if we dared in the slenderness of our ability to add something further to this admirable judgment, it would be to relate the characteristics of a prayer which, in our experience, is heard by the Lord.

32. 'When no hesitance interrupts us at prayer and destroys the confidence of our petition through some despair, and instead we perceive that we have obtained what we ask for by the very pouring forth of prayer, we do not doubt that our pleas have effectually made their way to God. That person will deserve to be heard and to succeed who believes that he is beheld by God and that God is able to accomplish it. This saying of Our Lord's cannot be repealed: "Whatever you seek in prayer, believe that you will receive it and it will come to you" [Mark 11:24].'

33. **GERMANUS**: 'Certainly we believe that this confidence of being heard comes from purity of conscience. But as for us, whose heart is even now pierced with sorrow by the thorn of sins, how can we have it? We have no merits advocating on our behalf, so that by them we might presume confidently that our prayers would be heard.'

34. **ISAAC**: (1) 'The message of the gospels and of the prophets teach us that there are different reasons for prayer being heard, in accordance with the different and varying condition of souls:

'You have the fruit of being heard marked out by our Lord's words in the case of two people in agreement, according to the passage, "If two of you shall agree upon earth concerning anything they shall ask for, it shall be done for them of my

Father who is in the heavens" [Matt. 18:19]. You have another in the fullness of faith, which is compared to a grain of mustard. "For if you have faith even like a grain of mustard," He says, "you shall say to this mountain: 'Be removed from this place', and it shall be removed; and nothing will be impossible for you" [Matt. 17:19]. (2) You have it in assiduousness with respect to prayer, which the Lord's word calls importunity because of the indefatigable persistence in petitioning: "Amen, I say unto you that, even if not because of his friendship, yet because of his persistence, he [the householder] will rise and give him as much as he needs" [Luke 11:8]. You have it in the fruit of almsgiving: "Store up alms in the heart of the poor and it shall pray for you in the time of tribulation" [Sir. 29:15]. You have it in the improvement of life and works of mercy, according to the passage, "Loose the bands of wickedness, undo the oppressing burdens"; (3) and after a few words in which the sterility of an unproductive fast is castigated, it is said, "Then you will call and the Lord will hear you; you will cry, and He will say, See, I am here" [Isa. 58:6, 9]. Sometimes an excess of distresses also causes it to be heard, according to the passage, "When I was distressed, I called upon the Lord, and He heard me" [Ps. 119:1]; and again: "Do not afflict the stranger, for if he cries out to Me I will hear him, since I am merciful" [Exod. 22:21, 27].

'So you see how many ways there are for the gift of being heard to be obtained, with the result that no one should be broken by his conscience's despair of attaining those things that are eternal and for salvation. (4) Suppose that, in contemplating our miseries, I concede that we are completely destitute of all those virtues which we considered above, having neither the commendable agreement of two persons, nor faith comparable to a grain of mustard, nor the works of piety that the prophet describes; even so, could we lack the persistence that He supplies to all who want it? It is for that persistence alone that the Lord promises to give whatever He has been petitioned to give. Therefore we ought to persevere in our requests without faithless hesitation, and never to doubt that if we continue in them we shall obtain all those things which we have asked that are appropriate to God.

(5) 'For the Lord, wishing to grant what is heavenly and eternal, exhorts us to compel Him (so to speak) by our persistence; not only does He not despise or reject the persistent, He actually welcomes, praises them, and most favourably promises to grant whatever they have persistently hoped for, saying, "Ask and you shall receive, seek and you shall find, knock and it shall be opened for you. For everyone who asks receives, and whoever seeks finds, and to the one who knocks it shall be opened" [Luke 11:9–10)]; and again, "All things whatever that you shall ask in prayer, believing, you shall receive, and nothing shall be impossible to you" [Matt. 21:22; 17:20]. (6) So then even if all the aforementioned reasons for being heard are altogether wanting, at least the steadfastness of persistence may quicken us, as this is given to anyone who wills—quite apart from any difficulties of merit or labour.

'But even when the suppliant doubts whether he has been heard, he should have no doubt that he certainly will be heard. We are taught by the example of the blessed Daniel that this also shall be sought from the Lord indefatigably, because, though he was heard on the first day when he began to pray, the result of his entreaty only followed after twenty-one days [cf. Dan. 10:2ff.]. (7) Therefore we, too, should not leave off once we undertake the purpose of our prayers, if we perceive that we are being heard rather slowly: perhaps the grace of being heard has been postponed by the Lord's providence for a good reason, or the angel of divine services, who was dispatched from the presence of the Almighty, has been detained in his departure by the resistance of the devil (for it is certain that he cannot force on us the desire of the gift conveyed, if he should discover that we have left off from the intention of the entreaty that we have purposed). This undoubtedly would have happened to the above mentioned prophet, too, but that with incomparable strength he prolonged the persistence of his prayers until the twenty-first day.

(8) 'So let us not be utterly broken by despair for want of confidence in this faith when we perceive that we have not obtained at all what we have prayed for, and let us not hesitate about the Lord's covenant, who says, "All things whatever that you shall ask in prayer, believing, you shall receive" [Matt. 21:22]. It is seemly for us to reconsider that saying of the blessed John the Evangelist, by which the ambiguity of this question is clearly resolved: "This is", he says, "the confidence which we have in Him, that whatever we ask according to His will, He hears us" [I John 5:14]. (9) He therefore bids us to have full and undoubting confidence of being heard only in matters conforming, not to our convenience or temporal consolations, but to the Lord's will. We are also taught to add this by the Lord's Prayer, where we say, "Your will be done"—Yours, not ours. If we also remember these words of the Apostle, that "we know not what to pray for as we ought" [Rom. 8:26], we shall understand that we sometimes petition for things contrary to our salvation and that we are most suitably refused what we have requested by Him who considers what is good for us more rightly and truly than we do.[33]

(10) 'There is no doubt this also befell the teacher of the Gentiles, when he prayed that that messenger of Satan (who had for his own good been allowed to buffet him by the Lord's will) would be removed from him, saying: "About this I pleaded with

the Lord three times that it might depart from me. And He said to me, 'My grace is sufficient for you, for strength is perfected in weakness'" [II Cor. 12:8-9]. Our Lord, too, expressed this sentiment when He prayed, in the person of His humanity,[34] that He might provide us with a form of prayer for other things by His example, when he said: "Father, if it is possible, let this cup pass from me; yet not as I will but as You will" [Matt. 26:39] – though of course His will was not discordant with the Father's will. (11) "For He had come to save what was lost, and give His soul a ransom for many" [Matt. 18:11; 20:28] – concerning which He Himself says: "No one takes My soul from Me, but I lay it down of Myself: I have the power to lay it down and I have the power to take it up again" [John 10:18]. About the unity of His will which He maintained with the Father, the following is sung in Psalm 39:[9] by the blessed David on behalf of this person: "I have willed, O My God, to do Your will".

'Even if we read about the Father, "For God loved the world in such a way that He gave His only begotten Son ..." [John 3:16], we find nonetheless about the Son, "Who gave Himself for our sins" [Gal. 1:4]. (12) And in the same way it is said about the former, "Who did not spare His own Son, but gave Him for all of us" [Rom. 8:32], it is also related about the latter, "He was offered because He Himself willed it" [Isa. 53:7]. So it is shown that the will of the Father and of the Son is one in all things: it is taught that even in the very mystery of the Lord's resurrection their working was not discordant. Just as the blessed Apostle preached that the Father accomplished the resurrection of His body, saying, "... and God the Father, who raised Him from the dead" [Gal. 1:11], so too the Son announced that He Himself will raise again the Temple of His body when He says, "Destroy this temple, and in three days I will raise it up again" [John 2:19].(13) 'And so having learned from the aforementioned examples of our Lord, we too ought to end our entreaties with like prayer and always to append this word to all our requests: "Nevertheless not as I will, but as You will" [Matt. 26:39]. But it is sufficiently clear that one who does not make a petition with an attentive mind cannot observe that threefold reverence which is usually celebrated in the assemblies of the brethren at the end of the service.[35]

35. (1) 'But before everything, that gospel precept must be most diligently observed, which tells us to enter our room, shut the door and pray to our Father [cf. Matt. 6:6]. This may be fulfilled by us as follows: we make our request within our room when, drawing our hearts within, away from the tumult of all thoughts and cares, we disclose our petitions to the Lord intimately and in secret. (2) We pray with the door closed when we pray with closed lips and total silence to the one who scrutinises not words, but hearts. We pray in secret when we reveal our requests to God alone from the heart and fervent mind, so that no hostile powers are able to recognize of what kind our petition is. (3) On this account, prayer should be made in complete silence, not only so that we do not distract the brethren standing nearby our whispers or cries and thus disturb the perceptions of those at prayer, but that the intention of our entreaty may be concealed from our enemies who particularly lie in ambush for us when we pray. Thus we shall fulfil this precept: "Guard the door of your mouth from her who sleeps in your bosom" [Mic. 7:5].

36. (1) 'For this reason prayer should be made frequently but briefly, lest our insidious enemy be able to implant something in our heart as we take our time about it.[36] For that is the true sacrifice, since "the sacrifice of God is a broken spirit" [Ps. 50:19]; this is the offering of salvation; these are pure libations; that is the "sacrifice of righteousness" [Ps. 50:21], the "sacrifice of

praise" [Ps. 49:23]; these are true and fat victims; they are "burnt offerings full of marrow" [Ps. 65:15] which are offered by broken and humble hearts—and when we offer them through the aforementioned control and fervour of spirit, we can sing with effectual power: "Let my prayer be set forth in Your sight as the incense, let the lifting up of my hands be an evening sacrifice" [Ps. 140:2]. (2) But the arrival of that very hour and of the night reminds us to render thanks with appropriate devotion, concerning which we seem to have put forth a great deal (from the measure of our slender ability) and to have prolonged our conference. And yet we believe that we have actually said little when compared to the loftiness and difficulty of the subject.'

More overwhelmed than satisfied by these words of the holy Isaac, we briefly rested our limbs after the evening service had been celebrated[37] and departed to our accommodation, intending at the crack of dawn to return with the promise of a fuller treatment, rejoicing as much over the acquisition of these precepts as over the assurance of his promises. We felt that, even though the excellence of prayer had been shown to us, we had not yet wholly understood from his words its nature and the power by which unbroken endurance in prayer could be gained and kept.

THE SECOND CONFERENCE OF ABBA ISAAC.

On Prayer

Contents

1. Introduction

2. On the custom which is observed in the province of Egypt for designating Easter

3. On Abbot Serapion and the heresy of the Anthropomorphites, which he contracted in the error of his simplicity

4. On our return to Abba Isaac, and a query concerning the error which the aforesaid elder committed

5. The answer regarding the origin of the heresy described above

6. On the reasons why Jesus Christ appears to each one of us either in His humility or in His glory

7. Wherein our end and perfect bliss consists

8. A question on the training in perfection through which we can arrive at perpetual recollection of God

9. The answer regarding the efficacy of understanding, which is gained through experience

10. On the instruction of continual prayer

11. On the perfection of prayer to which we can rise by the aforementioned system

12. A question as to how spiritual thoughts can be retained permanently

13. On the mobility of thoughts

14. The answer as to how stability of heart or of thoughts can be acquired

THE SEQUENCE of this narrative compels us to insert and find a place, amongst the lofty instructions of the anchorites that, by God's help, have been set forth (albeit in plain and unadorned style) for something which may seem to add a blemish to a fair body. I have no doubt, however, that by it no small instruction will be conferred on some rather simpler people in the matter of the image of Almighty God which we read about in Genesis—particularly when the foundations of such a doctrine are considered—since ignorance of it cannot but mean terrible blasphemy and harm to the Catholic faith.

2. (1) In the land of Egypt, this is the custom that is observed in keeping with ancient tradition: After the day of Epiphany (which the priests of that province regard as the time of our Lord's baptism and of His nativity according to the flesh as well, and so they celebrate the solemnity of either mystery on the single festival of this day and not separately as in the Western provinces), letters are sent from the bishop of Alexandria to all the churches of Egypt; by these letters, the beginning of Lent and the day of Easter are designated, not only in all the cities but also in all the monasteries.[38]

(2) Now, in keeping with this custom, just a few days after the previous conference with Abba Isaac had been held, the festal letters arrived from Theophilus, bishop of the aforesaid city.[39] In these letters, along with the announcement of Easter, he also argued against the Anthropomorphites' foolish heresy with an extended discussion, and refuted it in detail. This was received with such great bitterness by nearly the entire group of monks who dwell throughout the whole province of Egypt, because of their simplicity and error, that the greatest part of the elders decreed instead that the aforesaid bishop deserved to be condemned by the whole body of the brethren as one who had been tainted with the worst heresy: he seemed to attack the

teaching of Holy Scripture by denying that God Almighty was formed in the shape of a human figure (although in fact Scripture attests most clearly that Adam was created in His image). (3) Finally, this letter was rejected also by those who were living in the desert of Scetis, who excelled all who were in the monasteries of Egypt in perfection and in knowledge. Except for Abba Paphnutius, the priest of our congregation,[40] none of the priests who presided over the other three churches in the same desert would so much as allow it to be read or repeated in their meetings.

3. (1) There was amongst those who were captured by this mistaken notion a man named Serapion—a man of most ancient austerity and altogether perfected in asceticism,[41] whose ignorance in view of the aforementioned doctrine was injurious to all who maintained the true faith to the same extent that he himself surpassed nearly all the monks in the merits of his life and in the greatness of his age.

(2) Now when Serapion could not be brought back to the path of the right faith by many admonitions of the holy priest Paphnutius (in that this position seemed to him a novelty rather than something that had been taught or handed down by his predecessors), as it happened a certain deacon named Photinus, who was a man of profound learning, came from the region of Cappadocia out of a desire to visit the brethren living in the same desert. The blessed Paphnutius received him with the warmest welcome and, with a view to confirming the faith related in the letters of the previously mentioned bishop, placed him in the midst of the brethren and asked him before all of them how the Catholic churches of the East as a whole habitually interpreted the passage in Gen. [1:26] where it says, 'Let us make man after our image and likeness'.

(3) Now when he had explained that the 'image and likeness of God' was taken by all the leaders of the churches spiritually rather than according to the lowly sense of the letters, and he had proved in detail—with many examples from Scripture—that nothing of the sort could befall that infinite, incomprehensible and invisible majesty with the result that it could be encompassed in a human shape and likeness (since that which is by nature incorporeal, uncompounded and simple cannot be conceived by the mind any more than it can be detected by the eyes)—at last the old man, moved by this learned man's many powerful assertions, was drawn to the faith of the Catholic tradition.

(4) Abba Paphnutius (like the rest of us) was filled with unbounded delight at his assent, in that the Lord had not allowed a man of such great age who was perfected in so many virtues—one who erred only in ignorance and the simplicity of his lack of learning—to deviate from the path of right faith even to the end. But when we arose in thanksgiving and were all pouring forth prayers to the Lord, the old man's mind was confused during his prayer because he perceived that the anthropomorphic image of the Godhead that he habitually set before himself during prayer had been eliminated from his heart. Suddenly bursting into a flood of bitterest tears and choking sobs as a result, he cast himself down on the ground, exclaiming with powerful groans: 'Alas, wretch that I am [cf. Rom. 7:24]! (5) They have taken from me my God, Whom I would now grasp—but have not; Whom I would address or supplicate—but know no longer!'[42]

We were deeply disturbed by this and, with the effect of the previous conference lingering in our hearts, we returned to Abba Isaac. When we found him nearby, we addressed him with these words:

4. (1) 'Although our delight in the previous conference about the character of prayer would incite us to return to your Holiness and postpone everything else, quite apart from what has arisen lately, all the same this desire of ours is somewhat increased by Abba Serapion's grave error, which we suppose was conceived by the slyness of iniquitous demons. We are depressed by no small anguish when we consider him not only completely losing those labours which he has so laudably performed in the desert these fifty years, but also incurring the risk of eternal death, by the sin of this ignorance. (2) So first we want to know how and why such a grievous error has crept over him. Next, we ask to be taught how we can arrive at that quality of prayer that you spoke of some time ago, not only fully, but also splendidly. For that admirable conference has had on us the effect that it has only dazzled our minds, but not shown us how to accomplish or secure it.'

5. **ISAAC**: (1) 'No wonder if a really simple man who was never educated at all about the substance and nature of the Godhead could be restricted and deceived by the error of rusticity and the habit of a longstanding mistake and (to speak more truly) remain in the original mistake! But this mistake is introduced, not by a recent illusion of the demons as you thought but by the ignorance of the ancient paganism. In keeping with the custom of that mistake whereby they worshipped demons shaped in human forms, even now they reckon that the incomprehensible and ineffable majesty of the true Deity ought to be worshipped encompassed in some figure: for they believe that they can grasp or hold nothing if they have no image set before them, which they unceasingly call upon when they set themselves to pray, which they carry around in their minds, and which they always hold fixed before their eyes.

(2) 'This claim can be fittingly directed against their mistake: "And they changed the glory of the incorruptible God into the likeness of the image of corruptible man" [Rom. 1:23]. Jeremiah also says: "My people have changed their glory for an idol" [Jer. 2:11]. Although by its origin, of which we have spoken, this error was rooted in the senses of some, it is nevertheless also contracted in the spirits of those who have never been tainted with pagan superstition by the colour of the passage where it is said, "Let us make man in our image and our likeness" [Gen. 1:26], which ignorance and lack of learning have brought about. Thus, on account of this despicable interpretation, there has actually arisen the so-called Anthropomorphites' heresy, which with obstinate perversity contends that the endless simple substance of the Godhead is fashioned with our limitations and a human shape. (3) But anyone who has been informed in Catholic doctrine will abhor this as pagan blasphemy and thus will arrive at that perfectly pure kind of prayer which not only will not introduce into its petition any effigy or bodily limitations of the Godhead (which it is shameful even to mention!), but will not even allow in itself so much as the memory of a saying, the appearance of a deed, or the outline of any shape.

6. (1) 'As I said in the earlier conference, a given mind at prayer is elevated and formed according to the measure of its purity. The condition of its purity moves the mind along to the extent that it leaves off the contemplation of earthly and material things and enables Jesus to be seen with the inner gaze of the soul, either still humble and in the flesh or glorified and coming in the glory of His Majesty.[43] (2) Those who are still kept back in as it were a Jewish weakness are unable see Jesus coming in His Kingdom and cannot say with the Apostle: "And if we have known Christ according to the flesh, yet now we no longer know Him so" [II Cor. 5:16]. The only ones who can look upon His

Godhead with purest eye are those who, ascending from base and earthly works and thoughts, have sat with Him in the highest mountain of solitude which, free from all earthly thoughts, hidden from the tumult of passions and the contamination of all faults, and exalted by the purest faith and eminence of virtues, reveals the glory of His face and the image of His glory to those who deserve to gaze upon Him with the pure gaze of the soul. (3) Otherwise, Jesus is also seen by those who live in cities, towns and villages (i.e., who are occupied in the active life and works), but not with the same radiance with which He appeared to those who can go up into the aforesaid mount of the virtues with Him, namely, Peter, James and John [cf. Matt. 17:1].[44] Likewise, He appeared to Moses and spoke with Elias in solitude [cf. Exod. 3:2; 3 Kings 19:9 LXX].

(3) 'Our Lord, wishing to confirm this and leave us examples of perfect purity, withdrew alone into the mountain to pray [Matt. 14:23], even though He Himself as the very font of inviolable holiness did not need the benefit of external solitude or the help of withdrawal to obtain perfect purity (for the fullness of purity could not be stained by any of the crowds' filth, nor could He who cleanses and sanctifies all polluted things be contaminated by human interaction). In this way, He taught us by the example of His withdrawing that, if we wish to address God in a pure and spotless affection of heart, we should similarly withdraw from all the disturbance and chaos of the crowds so that, while still living in this body, we may fit ourselves in some degree to a likeness of that bliss which is promised hereafter to the saints and for us "God may be all in all" [I Cor. 15:28].

7. (1) 'Then our Saviour's prayer will be perfectly fulfilled in our case, for in praying for His disciples to the Father He said, "that the love with which You have loved Me may be in them, and they in Us;" and again: "that all may be one as You, Father,

in Me and I in You, that they also may be one in Us" [John 17:26, 21]. It will be fulfilled when that perfect love of God, with which "He first loved us" [I John 4:10], has passed into the feeling of our heart through the fulfilment of this prayer of the Lord's which we believe can in no way fail. (2) So it shall be, when our every love, desire, eagerness, effort and thought, all that we live, speak, breathe, will be God. And that unity which is now the Father's with the Son and the Son's with the Father will have transfused our perception and mind, that is, so that just as with a sincere and pure and indissoluble love He loves us, we too will be joined to Him by perpetual and inseparable delight, so linked to Him, to be sure, that whatever we breathe, understand, say, would be God. In Him, I say, we shall accomplish the end about which we spoke earlier, the which the Lord besought that it would be fulfilled in us when He prayed, "That they all may be one just as We are one, I in them and You in Me, that they too may be perfected in one" [John 17:22–3], and again, "Father, I wish that those whom You have given Me may themselves be with Me where I am" [John 17:22–4]. (3) So this should be the solitary's destination, this should be his entire aim so that he may be counted worthy to possess an image of the future blessedness even in this body and begin somehow to have a foretaste of a pledge of that heavenly life and glory in this vessel. This, I say, is the end of all perfection, so that every day the mind, purged from all carnal desires, may be lifted towards spiritual things, until its whole life and the heart's every thought are made one continuous prayer.'

8. **GERMANUS**: (1) 'The greatness of our astonishment at the awe-inspiring earlier conference (which is the reason we returned) is greatly increased! We fall into greater despair in the measure that we are fired with the desire of perfect blessedness by the inducements of this teaching, since we do not know how

to seek or obtain the discipline needed for such lofty heights. We therefore entreat you patiently to allow us to explain what we had begun to turn over in our minds as sitting in the cell we contemplated it at length (for perhaps it will be necessary to explain it with a good deal of talk); but we know that Your Blessedness is in no way offended by the infirmities of the weak, which for this very reason should be set out in the open, so that whatever is foolish in them may be corrected.

(2) 'Our opinion, then, is that it is necessary for the perfection of any art or discipline at all to begin with some simple rudiments and first be initiated with gentle and relatively easy beginnings so that, being nourished by rational milk (as it were) [cf. I Pet. 2:2] and trained little by little, it may grow and ascend from the depths to the heights by degrees and step by step. And when it has thus entered on the plainer principles and, so to speak, through the gates of profession that it has drawn near, it will consequently arrive without toil at the innermost and exalted peaks of perfection.

(3) 'For how could any boy manage to pronounce the simplest clusters of syllables, unless he had diligently learnt the letters of the alphabet? Or how can one who is still incompetent in linking short and simple sentences progress to reading quickly? By what means will one who is inadequately instructed in the science of grammar progress to rhetorical eloquence or philosophical knowledge? For this reason I have no doubt that there are some foundations to this loftiest discipline by which we are taught to adhere constantly to God; after these have been firmly laid, the exalted peaks of perfection may afterwards be also raised up upon them.

(4) 'And we tentatively suspect that these are its first principles: first, learn by which meditation God can be grasped

and considered; next, somehow be able to keep fast this subject (whatever it is) which we have no doubt stands as the pinnacle of all perfection. So we want to be shown some subject for this recollection by which God can be conceived and kept perpetually in the mind. Thus, keeping it before our eyes, we may have the wherewithal to recover ourselves and return at once when we sense that we have dropped away from it, and be able to resume it again without the difficult delay of wandering round and searching for it.

(5) 'Now it happens that, when we have returned to ourselves as if waking from a deadly sleep after wandering from spiritual *theoria*,[45] once we have been thoroughly roused we seek the subject by which we may be able to resurrect the spiritual recollection that has been destroyed, but before we find it we are held back by the delay of actually searching for it. So we are drawn aside from our effort once again and the purpose that was conceived in our hearts evaporates before the spiritual insight is born. It is sure enough that this confusion befalls us because we do not keep something special or some formula set firmly before our eyes, to which the wandering spirit may be recalled after many diversions and various digressions and, as it were, enter the port of silence after long storms.[46] (6) So it happens that the mind, which is constantly impeded by this ignorance and difficulty, is always cast about and wanders among various things as if it were drunk. It does not even hold firmly for any length of time to any of the spiritual things that may have occurred to it by chance rather than by its own effort, while it does not perceive the beginning and origin of them, or even their end and departure, since it is always receiving one thing after another.'

9. **ISAAC**: (1) 'Your very detailed and subtle inquiry offers an indication that purity is very near. For the only person who

would be able even to make inquiries on these matters (I will not say to look into them and make distinctions) is one whom diligent and effective mental labour and ever-vigilant concern had prompted to scrutinize the depths of these questions, one whom the continuous aim of a chaste life had by practical experience led to attempt the entrance to this purity and to knock at its doors. (2) And so since I see you, not standing before the doors of that true prayer which we have been discussing, but rather, touching its inner chambers and inward parts with the hands as it were of experience and already grasping some parts of it, I do not think that I shall find it too difficult now to introduce you who are already roaming around in the recesses, as the Lord may direct, into what I may call its hall. I also do not think that you will be held back by the obstacle of any difficulty from investigating the things that will be shown you. (3) For one who prudently recognizes what he should ask is near to understanding, nor is one far from knowledge who begins to understand what he does not know. So I am not afraid of being accused of indiscretion and frivolity if I divulge the things that I had refrained from discussing when speaking in my former treatment of the perfection of prayer. I think that its force was to be reserved for you who are occupied with this subject and with asceticism, even without the service of my speech, by the grace of God.[47]

10. (1) 'Therefore in accordance with that instruction which you have with insight compared to teaching children (who are not able to understand the first lessons of the alphabet and cannot recognize the shapes of the letters and trace their characters with a steady hand other than by accustoming themselves to make their figures by continually contemplating and daily imitating some examples and shapes that have been carefully impressed on wax), the formula of this spiritual *theoria*

must also be handed down to you. Always focusing your gaze with utmost steadiness on it, you may both learn to roll it round in your mind profitably with uninterrupted continuity and you may be able, by practising and meditating upon it, to ascend to an even loftier insight.

(2) 'This formula of the discipline which you seek, and of prayer shall therefore be proposed to you, which every monk who progresses towards continual recollection of God is used to meditating upon in the ceaseless revolving of his heart, once all kinds of other thoughts have been expelled (for he cannot possibly retain it unless he has been released from all bodily cares and concerns). In the same way that it was handed down to us by a few of the most ancient fathers who were still alive, likewise it is only made known by us to a very few who are really keen. So then this pious formula for possessing the perpetual recollection of God will be set before you: "O God, come unto my aid; O Lord, hasten to help me" [Ps 69:2]. (3) Not unreasonably has this brief verse been picked out from the whole body of Scripture, for it admits of all the feelings which can arise in human nature, and can be adapted to every situation and all assaults fittingly and satisfactorily. It has an invocation of God against every danger, it has the humility of a pious confession, it has the vigilance of concern and continual fear, it has the consideration of one's own frailty, the confidence of being heard, and the assurance of a present and ever ready protection. (4) (For one who constantly calls on his protector is certain that He is always ready.) It has the ardour of love and charity, it has an understanding of the schemes of the enemy and a dread of them, because of which, one who perceives that he is surrounded by them day and night confesses that he cannot be freed without the aid of his defender.

'This brief verse is an impregnable wall, and impenetrable defence and a most strong shield for all those who labour under the disturbance of demons. It does not allow those who are fixed in *akedia* and anxiety of mind,[48] or who are depressed by sadness or all kinds of thoughts, to despair of saving remedies since it shows that He whom it invokes is continually looking on at our struggles and is not far from His suppliants. (5) It admonishes us who have established some spiritual success and delight of heart not to be elated at all or puffed up by our happy situation (which it attests cannot last without God as our protector) even as it implores Him to help us not only continually but also speedily.

'This brief verse, I say, will be found helpful and useful to each one of us in whatever condition of life. For one who wants to be helped always and in everything shows that he needs God as his helper, not only in sorrowful or harsh matters, but equally in favourable and happy ones, in order to be delivered from the former and also made to abide in the latter, since he knows that human weakness can endure in neither of them without His assistance.

(6) 'I am afflicted by the passion of gluttony: I ask for food unknown in the desert, and in the filthy wilderness, odours of royal dishes waft to me and I perceive that very much against my will I am drawn to long for them—I must at once say, "O God, come unto my aid; O Lord, hasten to help me". I am goaded to take something before the time appointed for supper, or I am attempting with great sorrow in my heart to keep to the due measure of right and customary meagreness—I must cry out with groans: "O God, come unto my aid; O Lord, hasten to help me". (7) Weariness of the stomach prohibits me from stricter fasting on account of the assaults of the flesh, or a parched belly and constipation deters me; for my wishes to be granted, or else for the agitation of carnal lust to be quenched without the

measure of a stricter fast, I must pray: "O God, come unto my aid; O Lord, hasten to help me". Upon coming to supper when the proper time arrives, I abhor the bread and am kept from eating anything to satisfy the requirements of nature—I must cry with a wail: "O God, come unto my aid; O Lord, hasten to help me".

(8) 'When I want to apply myself to reading for the sake of the heart's stability, the onset of a headache keeps me from it, my drowsy head falls upon the sacred page at the third hour and I am compelled either to violate or to anticipate the allocated time for rest; in the end, an unbearable attack of sleepiness drives me to cut short the canonical rule for the synaxis and the Psalter[49]—I must likewise cry out: "O God, come to unto my aid; O Lord, hasten to help me". Rest is taken from my eyes, for many nights I see myself shattered from diabolical dreams, and all the repose of nightly rest is kept from my eyelids—I must pray with sighs: "O God, come unto my aid; O Lord, hasten to help me".

(9) 'Even as I am in the midst of a struggle with sins, a fleshly titillation strikes me unexpectedly and tries with a delightful caress to bring me to consent as I sleep[50]—lest a blazing fire from without consume the fragrant flowers of chastity, I must cry out: "O God, come unto my aid; O Lord, hasten to help me". I perceive that the incentive to lust is extinguished and that the sexual heat in my members has died down—in order that the virtue that has been born, or rather this grace of God, may abide with me longer, indeed forever, I must intently say: "O God, come unto my aid; O Lord, hasten to help me".

(10) 'I am distressed by the pangs of anger, covetousness and sadness and compelled to interrupt the peaceful state that was established and dear to me—lest I be carried off into the bitterness of gall by a raging perturbation, I must cry out with

groans from my inner being: "O God, come unto my aid; O Lord, hasten to help me". I am tempted with being carried away by *akedia,* vainglory and pride as my mind flatters itself somewhat with a subtle thought of the negligence and indifference of others—lest this pernicious suggestion of the enemy overcome me, I must pray with all contrition of heart: "O God, come unto my aid; O Lord, hasten to help me". (11) I have acquired the grace of humility and simplicity, having got rid of the tumour of pride by continually mortifying my spirit—lest the "foot of pride come against me and the hand of the sinner move me" [Ps. 35:12] again and I be confounded all the more seriously by being carried away at my success, I must cry out with all my strength, "God, come unto my aid; O Lord, hasten to help me".

'I am ablaze with countless different wanderings of soul and with instability of heart, I am not able to control my scattered thoughts, I cannot even pour forth my prayer without interruption, apparitions of meaningless figures, and the remembrance of conversations and deeds, and I sense that I am constricted by such dryness and sterility that I feel I cannot give birth to any offspring of spiritual perceptions—in order that I may be vouchsafed to be set free from this filthiness of mind, from which I cannot extricate myself by many sighs and groans, I shall necessarily cry out: "O God, come unto my aid; O Lord, hasten to help me".

(12) 'Again, I sense that at the visitation of the Holy Spirit I have gained direction of soul, stability of thoughts and keenness of heart with ineffable joy and transport of mind,[51] and in the superabundance of spiritual perceptions I have perceived a revelation of most holy ideas which had previously been altogether hidden from me to overflow at a sudden illumination from the Lord. In order that I may be vouchsafed to dwell longer

in them, I must anxiously and frequently exclaim: "O God, come unto my aid; O Lord, hasten to help me".

(13) 'Surrounded by nightly terrors of demons, I am agitated and I am distressed by apparitions of unclean spirits, my very hope of salvation and life is withdrawn with a shudder of fear—flying to the safe haven of this verse, I will cry out with all strength: "O God, come unto my aid; O Lord, hasten to help me". Again, when I have been renewed by the Lord's consolation and, enlivened by His coming, I sense that I am encompassed as if by innumerable thousands of angels, so that I suddenly dare to seek the fight and provoke a conflict with those whom I dreaded worse than death before and whose touch (or even approach!) I felt with a shudder of mind and body—in order that by God's grace the vigour of this perseverance may dwell even longer in me, I must cry out with all my strength: "O God, come unto my aid; O Lord, hasten to help me".

(14) 'The prayer of this verse must be poured forth with unceasing constancy: in adversity, so that we are delivered; in prosperity, so that we are preserved and not puffed up. Let the meditation of this verse, I tell you, be revolved in your breast without interruption. You should not stop chanting it, regardless of what work, office or travel you find yourself in. Meditate on it when you are sleeping, eating and in the basic necessities of nature. May this pondering in your heart, once it has become like a formula of salvation, not only protect you unharmed from every attack of the demons, but also lead you to those invisible and heavenly *theories*, purifying you from all sins by earthly pollution, and so carry you on to that ineffable ardour of prayer experienced by very few. (15) Let sleep overtake you meditating upon this verse until, having been shaped by incessantly practising it, you are accustomed to repeating it even in your sleep. Let it be the first thing that occurs to you when you

awaken, let it go before all your waking thoughts, let it put you on your knees when you rise from bed and send you on from there to all your work and actions; let it follow you all the time. You shall meditate upon this, in keeping with the Lawgiver's precepts, "at home and walking on a journey", [Deut. 6:7] sleeping and waking. You shall write it on the threshold and door of your mouth, you shall place it upon the walls of your home and the inner places of your heart, so that it may be your chant when you are kneeling on your knees to pray and it may become your constant and established prayer when you rise from there and set out on all the necessary business of life.

11. (1) 'This, this is the formula which the mind should hold to incessantly until, fortified by constantly using and continually meditating upon it, it casts off and rejects the rich and full resources of all thoughts and so, having restricted itself to the poverty of this one verse, comes through with ready ease to that beatitude of the gospel which holds the first place among the other beatitudes. For it says, "Blessed are the poor in spirit, for theirs is the kingdom of heaven" [Matt. 5:3]. So one who emerges as a distinguished pauper by this sort of poverty will fulfil this saying of the prophet: "The poor and needy shall praise the name of the Lord" [Ps. 73:21]. (2) And indeed what greater or holier poverty can there be than this? For by this poverty, a man knows that he has no defence and no personal strength, asks for daily help from another's liberality and, being aware that every single moment his life and substance depend on divine succour, admits not unreasonably that he is truly the Lord's beggar and cries to Him daily by way of petition, "But I am poor and needy: the Lord helps me" [Ps. 39:18 LXX].

'Ascending to the manifold knowledge of God by God's own illumination, one begins henceforward to be fattened on loftier and holier mysteries, in keeping with what was said by the prophet, "The high hills are a refuge for the stags, the rocks for the hedgehogs" [Ps 103:18]. This saying is used very satisfactorily in the sense we have given, in that whoever perseveres in simplicity and innocence is injurious or harmful to no one but, being content with his own simplicity, merely wishes to protect himself from those who lie in ambush for him. So having become as it were a spiritual hedgehog, one is protected by the continual covering of that gospel rock which is the memory of the Lord's passion and, defended by ceaseless meditation on the aforesaid verse, one escapes from the snares of the enemy lying in wait. Of these spiritual hedgehogs, we read in Proverbs [30:26] as follows: "And the hedgehogs are a feeble race, who have made their homes in the rocks". (4) What indeed is feebler than a Christian, what is weaker than a monk? Not only is no vengeance allowed to the monk for any of his injuries, but not even a mild and slight annoyance is permitted to spring up within him.

'One who not only retains the simplicity of innocence when advancing from this condition but also, shielded by the virtue of discretion, becomes an exterminator of deadly serpents— having Satan crushed beneath his feet—and by his mental alacrity has attained to the figure of the rational stag, will graze on the mountains of the prophets and Apostles, that is, on their most excellent and loftiest mysteries. Flourishing on this constant grazing, once he receives into himself all of the Psalms' emotional responses[52] he will begin to sing them as if they were not composed by the psalmist, but instead were his own production. It is as if he were drawing forth his own prayer with deep compunction of heart; certainly, he will reckon that the Psalms are directed at himself and understand that their words were not fulfilled only then by the prophet or in the prophet, but they are born and fulfilled daily in him.

(5) 'For the Holy Scriptures then are disclosed to us more clearly and as it were their veins and marrow are exposed, when our experience not only perceives but even anticipates their inner meaning, and the sense of the words is unlocked for us not by explanation but by proof. For receiving the actual emotional response of heart in which each psalm was sung and written, becoming as it were their authors, we anticipate the meaning rather than follow it. That is, gathering the force of the things said before knowing them, we recall what has happened to us and what is happening in daily assaults when we meditate upon them. While we sing them we recollect what our negligence has produced for us or our diligence has procured and divine providence has gathered together; or what the enemy's instigation has deprived us of, what slippery and subtle forgetfulness has taken away and human frailty has brought about, or irresponsible ignorance has cheated us of.

(6) 'We find all these emotional responses expressed in the Psalms so that, by seeing the things that happen as it were in the clearest mirror, we understand them better. Thus, instructed by the teaching of our emotional responses, we feel our way through them as things that we have seen and not just heard; from the deep emotional responses of the heart, we give birth to what is implanted in the very nature of things and not simply what has been commended to our memory, so that we penetrate to their meaning by anticipating it through experience and not simply by reading the text. Thus, our mind will arrive at that incorruptible prayer to which the argument of our conference ascended—insofar as the Lord deigns to provide it—in the previous treatment.[53] Not only is this prayer not engaged with gazing on any image, in fact it is not even enunciated by any sequence of words or sounds; by the fiery purpose of the mind, it is produced through the ineffable transport of the heart with an

insatiable keenness of spirit and the mind, being thus brought beyond all the senses and visible material, pours forth this prayer to God "with unutterable groans" [cf. Rom. 8:26] and sighs.'

12. **GERMANUS**: 'We think that not only the tradition of this spiritual discipline (about which we asked) has been handed down by you, but also perfection itself—and that quite openly and clearly. For what can be more perfect, what more lofty than for the memory of God to be encompassed in such an abridged meditation, to move beyond the limits of the visible by rolling around a single verse, and to include in one short saying the emotional responses of all our prayers?[54] Therefore we beg you now to explain to us one remaining point: how we can hold fast to this verse which you have handed down to us as a formula in such a way that, just as by God's grace we have been freed from the follies of worldly thoughts, we may likewise firmly retain all spiritual ones?

13. (1) 'For when the mind conceives of the meaning of any Psalm, it turns to the text of another scripture in stupid ignorance as the first one imperceptibly slips away. And when it has begun to consider the latter within itself, the recollection of some other passage cuts off the meditation on the previous material even though it has not been thoroughly aired. It is also transferred from this to something else when another meditation sneaks in; and so the soul always whirls round from psalm to psalm, jumps from a text in the gospel to a reading from the Apostle, wheels round from here to the prophetic writings and is carried away from there to some spiritual histories: in this way, it is cast about, unstable and aimless, through the whole body of the Scriptures. Being able by its own will to reject or retain nothing or to complete anything with a full consideration and

examination, it has become merely one who touches and tastes of spiritual meanings, not a creator and possessor of them.

(2) 'Thus the mind, ever aimless in its movement even at the time of the synaxis—as though it were drunk—is distracted by all kinds of things and performs none of the offices properly. For instance, when it prays, it recalls some psalm or reading; when it chants, it meditates on something other than what the text of the psalm itself contains; when it reads a lesson, it wishes it were doing something or remembers something it has done. Thus taking and rejecting nothing in a disciplined and appropriate way, it is seen to be driven by chance events, not having the power to retain the things that delight it or dwell upon them. (3) It is therefore necessary for us to know above all how we can complete these spiritual offices properly and indeed keep firmly this very verse, the form of which you have handed down to us, so that the beginnings and ends of our perceptions may not fluctuate with their rapid variations but may remain under our authority.'

14. **ISAAC**: (1) 'Although enough was, as it seems to me, expressed on this matter in our former discussions about the status of prayer, since you nevertheless ask for it to be repeated to you, I will instruct you briefly concerning securing one's heart. There are three things which make an aimless mind stable: vigils, meditation and prayer; diligence and constant purpose in them will confer stable firmness upon the soul.[55] (2) And yet this cannot be possessed in any other way unless all concerns and cares of the present life have been first renounced through indefatigable constancy in work dedicated not to covetousness but to the sacred practices of the monastery. Thus we may be able to fulfil the apostolic command, "Pray without ceasing" [I Thess. 5:17]. Whoever is used to praying only at such time as the knee is bent, prays very little. But whoever, even on bended

knee, is distracted by any sort of wandering heart, prays not at all. And for this reason, it behoves us even before the time of prayer to be such as we would wish to be found at prayer. For it is necessary that the mind be formed at the time of its supplication by its previous condition; and by those thoughts on which it had tarried before prayer, its prayer is either elevated to heavenly things or else plunged into earthly things.'

(3) Abba Isaac related his second conference on the quality of prayer to this point, and we were astonished. We greatly admired his teaching about meditation on the aforementioned verse (which he handed down to be retained by beginners by way of an outline) and strongly wished to cultivate it , as we believed that it would be brief and easy—but we have experienced it to be rather more difficult to observe than that asceticism of ours by which before we used to scurry through the whole body of scriptures by inconstant meditation without the chain of any perseverance. So it is settled that absolutely nobody is excluded from perfection of heart by being unable to read nor does rusticity hinder laying hold of purity of heart and mind, which is extremely near to all, if only they will, with constant meditation on this verse, keep the mind's whole and intact purpose fixed on God.

NOTES

[1] The standard English biography remains the second edition of Owen Chadwick's *John Cassian* (Cambridge: CUP, 1968); more comprehensive, but less widely available, is Leon Cristiani's *Jean Cassien* (Abbaye S. Wandrille: Editions de Fontenelle, 1946). Also eminently worth reading is Columba Stewart's *Cassian the Monk* (New York: OUP, 1998).

[2] On this aspect of Cassian's writings, there is an important contribution by Columba Stewart, 'From *logos* to verbum: John Cassian's Use of Greek in the Development of Latin Monastic Vocabulary', in *The Joy of Learning and the Love of God: Studies in Honor of Jean Leclercq*, edited by E. Rozanne Elder (Kalamazoo MI: Cistercian Publications, 1995) 5-31.

[3] See Ferrandus, *Life of Fulgentius* 12.24 (PL 65: 128-29).

[4] Prosper of Aquitaine, for instance, attacked Cassian savagely (and incompetently): see A. Casiday, 'Rehabilitating John Cassian: An evaluation of Prosper of Aquitaine's critique of "Semipelagianism"', in the *Scottish Journal of Theology* 58, no. 3 (2005): 270–84.

[5] For instance, J.-C. Guy, 'Jean Cassien, historien du monachisme égyptien?' *Studia Patristica* 8 (1966), pp. 366-72; K. S. Frank, 'John Cassian on John Cassian,' *Studia Patristica* 30 (1996) 418-33.

[6] See Cassian, *Institutes*, Preface, 8-9.

[7] See H. G. Evelyn-White, *The Monasteries of the Wâdi 'n Natrûn, part II: The History of the Monasteries of Nitria and of Scetis* (New York: The Metropolitan Museum, 1932) 125-44 and, for a more recent and theoretically informed approach, E. A. Clark, *The Origenist Controversy: The Cultural Construction of an Early Christian Debate* (Princeton, NJ: Princeton University Press, 1992).

[8] I have only found Cassian to use the expression *ipsa verba* (the 'very words') three times in the whole of his corpus: *Conferences* 8.23 and 9.13, *Incarnation* 4.2. But the old chestnut about whether it is reasonable to suppose that Cassian is relating the precise words of the abbas at a remove of roughly thirty years is ill-considered. Cassian's aim seems rather to have been more like that of Thucidydes, in his *History* A.

1.22.1: '... it has been difficult to recall the precise words of the speeches that I listened to myself—and it is likewise with my informants. So each person shall say concerning the situation at hand what is, in my view, most necessary, while I keep close to the complete sense of what was actually said.'

[9] A good example of this kind of sensitive evaluation of Cassian's writings is available in Adalbert de Vogüé, 'Pour comprendre Cassien. Un survoi des Conferences,' *Collectanea Cisterciensia* 39 (1977) 250-72.

[10] See C. Stewart, *Cassian the Monk*, pp. 136-37 and especially J-C. Guy, '2. Isaac (les Isaac moines d'Égypte). 3. Isaac, prêtre des Cellules,' in the *Dictionnaire de Spiritualité*, 7.II, 2005-06.

[11] On these monks, see now Mark Sheridan, 'The Spiritual and Intellectual World of Early Egyptian Monasticism', *Coptica* 1 (2002)1-51.

[12] See Brian Daley, 'What did "Origenism" mean in the Sixth Century?' in *Origeniana Sexta*, edited by Gilles Dorival and Alain le Boulleuc (Leuven: Peeters, 1995) 627-38.

[13] See René Draguet, 'L'Histoire lausiaque, une œuvre écrite dans l'esprit d'Évagre', *Revue d'histoire ecclésiastique* (1946-1947) 41-42 321-64, pp. 5-49.

[14] See S. Marsili, *Giovanni Cassiano ed Evagrio Pontico: Dottrina sulla Carità e Contemplazione* (Rome: Editrice Anselmiana, 1936).

[15] E.g. Cristian Bădiliţă has hypothesized (rather fancifully, in my view) that Abba Serenus of *Conferences* 7 and 8 is in fact Evagrius: 'Plusieurs indices nous font supposer que sous les traits psychologiques et intellectuels de Serenus (celui qui est devenu un *apathes*) se cacherait Evagre lui-même, le grand absent de l'œuvre de Cassien. Mais la démonstration de cette identification reste à faire'. See his 'Jean Cassien et le mythe des anges déchus', in *Jean Cassien entre l'orient et l'occident*, eds Bădiliţă and Attila Jakab (Paris: Beauchesne, 2003) 221-37 at 221 n 2.

[16] See, e.g. G. Bunge, 'Evagre le Pontique et les deux Macaire', *Irénikon* 56 (1983) 215-27, 323-60; J. Driscoll, 'Exegetical procedures in the desert monk Poemen', in *Mysterium Christi: Symbolgegenwart und theologische Bedeutung*, edited by M. Lobrer and E. Salmann (Rome: Sant' Anselmo,

1995) 155-78; *idem*, 'Evagrius and Paphnutius on the causes for abandonment by God', *Studia Monastica* 39 (1997) 259-86; *idem*, 'The Fathers of Poemen and the Evagrian Connection', *Studia Monastica* 42 (2000) 27-51.

[17] For further considerations on Cassian's teaching of deification, see my paper, 'Deification in Origen, Evagrius and Cassian', in *Origeniana Octava*, edited by L. Perrone (Leuven: Peeters, 2003) 995-1001.

[18] See *Institutes* 2.9.1.

[19] Cassian calls Castor and Leon 'papae' (whence, 'popes'), but this means no more than 'bishops'.

[20] Cf. Evagrius, *On prayer* 2: 'A soul purified by the fullness of the commandments prepares a steadfast organisation for the mind, making it receptive of the desired state.' (All translations from Evagrius are taken from my volume in the Early Church Fathers series, *Evagrius Ponticus* (London: Routledge, 2006).

[21] Cf. Evagrius, *On prayer* 70: 'Stand guard, protecting your mind from representations at the time of prayer, and make your stand on your own state of rest so that he who sympathises with the ignorant may also regularly visit you and then you may get the most glorious gift of prayer.'

[22] Already, Cassian intimates that the goals of virtue are *contemplatio Dei* and *spirituales intuitus*, which corresponds precisely to Evagrius' teaching. See Salvatore Marsili, *Giovanni Cassiano ed Evagrio Pontico*, Studia Anselmiana 5 (Rome, 1936) 38-41, 61-65, 121-144.

[23] Cf. Evagrius, *Gnostic Chapters* II, 6 (PO 28.62-3): 'The ascetic soul which, by God's grace, has conquered and departed from the body will be in those regions of knowledge where the wings of its impassibility will take it.'

[24] The description of demons as 'Ethiopians' is, regrettably, quite common in the literature. See, in the *Apophthegmata: Alphabetic Collection*, Heraclides; in the *Anonymous Collection* (published by J-C. Guy, *Recherche sur la tradition grecque des Apophthegmata Patrum* (Brussels 1962)), N173(41), N426, N596; Daniel of Scetis 10, N628;

ps.-Rufinus, *Vitae Patrum* 3.43 (PL 73.739-810); Paulos Evergetinos, *Synagoge* 3.16.7.3 (Athens, 1997), III, 211; Palladius, *Lausiac History* 23.5; *Historia Monachorum in Aegypto* 8.4; Cassian, *Conference* 2.10-13.

[25] Cf. Origen, *On Prayer,* 12.2 (ed. Koetschau (1899), 1.324.25-325.3): 'He prays "without ceasing" who unites prayer to the necessary deeds and fitting actions to prayer, since virtuous deeds or fulfilling the commandments are included as a part of prayer; for we can only accept the command to "pray without ceasing" as meaning something possible if we mean that the saint's whole life taken together is one great prayer.'

[26] The word translated here 'perceptions' is *sensuum*, which derives from *sentire*—a Latin verb that refers to feeling, sensing and perceiving. The noun has a similar range of meaning, with the result that some translators (e.g. Gibson) take it as referring to an emotional experience and others (e.g. Chadwick, Degli Innocenti, Ramsey) emphasise the intellectual aspect of the word.

[27] The word here translated 'struck with sorrow' is *compunctus*, which is an important term in Christian ascetical literature; though it is now dated in some of its particulars; I. Hausherr's *Penthos: the doctrine of compunction in the Christian East,* trans. A. Hufstader (Kalamazoo, MI: Cistercian Publications 1982), is still a fundamental study of the term. See also Barbara Müller, *Der Weg des Weinens: Die Tradition des "Penthos" in den Apophthegmata Patrum* (Göttingen: Vandenhoeck and Ruprecht, 2000).

[28] Cassian is relating a specifically Evagrian gloss of prayer (*proseuchê*) as vow (*euchê*). Cf. Evagrius, *Capita cognoscitiva* 16 (ed. Muyldermans: 'Evagriana,' *Le Muséon* 44 (1931) 37-68, here at 53): 'Prayer is the voluntary offering of goods'. (For 'prayer', I follow Barberini in reading *euchê* for *psuchê*.) For further discussion, see S. Marsili, *Giovanni Cassiano ed Evagrio Pontico* (Rome: Sant' Anselmo, 1936) 98-100, n. 2.

[29] Cf. Evagrius, *Capita cognoscitina* 19 (ed. Muyldermans: 53): 'Intercession is the advocacy before God of the superior for the sake of others' salvation.'

[30] This explanation of what it means to be 'equal to the angels' [cf. Luke 20:36] can be compared to Gregory of Nyssa, *On the making of man* 17 (PG 44: 188-9) and Evagrius, *On prayer* 113: 'Through true prayer, the monk becomes "equal to the angels" [Luke 20:36], yearning to "see the face of the Father who is in heaven"' [Matt. 18:10].

[31] It should be noted that this is being said in precisely such a 'spiritual conversation' (*conlatio spiritalis*).

[32] Cf. Evagrius, *Causes for monastic observances* 9: 'And groan, weep and put on the form of mourning for the judgment of sinners, fearing lest you yourself also be numbered among them. But rejoice, exult and be glad at the good things that have been set aside for the righteous. Exert yourself to enjoy the latter, but avoid the former.'

[33] Cf. Evagrius, *On prayer* 32, 89: 'Often in praying I requested that what seemed good to me would be done and persisted in my request, irrationally contending with God's will and not yielding to him so that he would providentially arrange what he knew to be more expedient. And in the event when I finally got it, I was deeply disappointed that I had requested instead that my own desire be done, for the thing did not turn out to be for me such as I had reckoned'; 'Do not want for your affairs to transpire as seems best to you, but as pleases God, and you will be undisturbed and thankful in your prayer.'

[34] Cassian often uses the expression here translated as 'humanity' (Latin: *homo assumptus,* 'assumed man') in describing the Lord's humanity (e.g. *Institutes* 12.17; *Conferences* 7.22, 9.34.10, 16.6.4, 22.12.1; *On the Incarnation* 1.2.5, 1.5.4, 2.3.10, 2.6.1, 5.6.3—though most of these passages are actually citations from another author). And he has been faulted for doing so by modern scholars; see for instance A. Grillmeier, *Christ in the Christian Tradition, Vol. I: From the Apostolic Age to Chalcedon* (451), trans. John Bowden. (Atlanta: John Knox Press, 1975) 468; Stewart, *Cassian the Monk,* 23. This expression was part of a precise Christology that was advanced by Theodore of Mopsuestia (see his *On the Incarnation 7,* ed. Swete, 296-98) and was condemned in 553 (see canons 12 and 13 of Constantinople II, ed. Straub, 218-19). But the term was widely used by Cassian's contemporaries (for instance, Apponius,

On the Song of Songs 3.3, 5.32, 9.47, 12.12, 12.46, 12.50 [CCSL 19: 61, 130, 233, 273, 288, 290], Hilary of Poitiers, *On the Trinity* 1.11,13, 16, 2.25 *et passim* [PL 10: 33-34, 36, 67] and Augustine, *Letters* 137.2.6, 137.4.14, 140.3.9, 148.2.10, 148.4.15, 169.2.8, 187.13.39-40, 238.3.18 [CSEL 44: 103-05, 116-17, 161, 340-41, 344-45, 617; 57: 116-18, 546-47]. In fact, Latin authors commonly used the concrete noun 'man/*homo*' instead of the abstract noun 'humanity/*humanitas*': see Donald Fairbairn, *Grace and Christology in the Fifth-Century Church* (Oxford: OUP, 2003) 190-92. We might therefore think it a bit churlish for Cassian to come in for criticism in respect of a widely attested usage.

[35] This is a difficult passage and some (notably, Chadwick, *John Cassian*: p. 50) have even suggested that it is an interpolation. There is, however, no support for this suggestion in the manuscript tradition. It should be noted, however, that for this translation I follow the variant reading 'qui intento animo *non* supplicat' ('who does *not* make a petition with an attentive mind') which makes rather more sense than the reading given by Petschenig *et al*: 'qui intento animo supplicat' ('who makes a petition with an attentive mind').

[36] Frequent and brief prayer is a staple of Egyptian monastic spirituality; see, e.g. Evagrius, *On prayer* 98: 'In the time of such temptations, make use of brief, intense prayer'; and *Refutations* (also known by the Greek title, *Antirrhetikos), passim;* cf. G. Bunge '"Priez sans cesse". Aux origins de la prière hésychaste', *Studia Monastica* 30 (1998), 7-16. Such prayers are often called 'monologistic' in the tradition, because they are precisely focused. The most famous monologistic prayer is the Jesus Prayer, which is perhaps best known from the anonymous classic, *The Way of the Pilgrim* but which has its roots in Egyptian practice (see Antoine Guillaumont, 'Jesus Prayer among the Monks of Egypt', *Eastern Churches Review* 6 (1974), 66-71).

[37] It should not escape our attention that Cassian concludes his account of the conference by relating that those present participated in the evening service—an act of corporate prayer.

[38] The first bishop to disseminate these festal letters was Dionysius (*c*.247-64), according to Eusebius' *Ecclesiastical History*, 7.10-11, 20-22.

The custom was well established by Cassian's time. The festal letters written by Athanasius have attracted a considerable amount of scholarly attention: see now Alberto Camplani, *Atanasio di Alessandria. Lettere festali. Anonimo. Indice delle lettere festali* (Milan: Paoline, 2003), with an excellent discussion of the place of festal letters in the Egyptian church.

[39] As mentioned in the introduction, Theophilus was subsequently to turn his attention to the opponents of the 'Anthropomorphites' and drive them from Egypt. He has often been accused of opportunism for this, not least by the ancient church historians Sozomen (see his *Historia Ecclesiastica* 8.11-12 [PG 67. 1544-49]) and Socrates (*Historia Ecclesiastica* 6.7 [PG 67. 684-88]). For a modern attempt to vindicate Theophilus, see Norman Russell, 'Theophilus and Cyril of Alexandria on the divine image. A consistent episcopal policy toward the Origenism of the desert?' in *Origeniana Octava*, edited by Lorenzo Perrone (Leuven: Leuven University Press and Peeters, 2003) 939-46.

[40] For the role of the 'priest of the congregation' during this time, see the valuable discussion in Evelyn White's reconstruction of the organization of Kellia: Hugh G. Evelyn White, *The Monasteries of the Wâdi 'n Natrûn, part II: The History of the Monasteries of Nitria and of Scetis* (New York: The Metropolitan Museum, 1932) 175-78.

[41] For a comparison of Cassian to Evagrius in regard to *praktikê* (here translated as 'asceticism'), see Marsili, *Giovanni Cassiano ed Evagrio Pontico,* 110-15.

[42] Cf. the austere admonition of Evagrius, *On prayer* 67: 'Never give a shape to the divine as such when you pray, nor allow your mind to be imprinted by any form, but go immaterial to the Immaterial and you will understand.'

[43] Origen put forward the idea that the Lord appears in different ways to different people in his *Against Celsus* 2.64, 4.16 and 6.77—and it may be more than coincidental that, in those passages, Origen connects the teaching to the Transfiguration (much as Cassian does here). See further John McGuckin, 'The Changing Forms of Jesus', in *Origeniana*

Quarta, ed. Lothar Lies (Innsbruck and Vienna: Tyrolia-Verlag, 1987) 215-22.

[44] The scriptural image of the Transfiguration is central to Isaac's (and therefore Cassian's) description of pure prayer—and so his reference to the 'radiance' of Christ's appearance can be seen to be in continuity with the light mysticism that is more widely attested in Evagrius' works, *pace* O. Chadwick, *John Cassian* (Cambridge: CUP, 1950) 148. Since the contemplation of Christ's radiant appearance in this account corresponds to the vision of light in Evagrius' works, it is not surprising that other elements of Isaac's description of the ascent of Mount Olivet (e.g. leaving off 'the contemplation of earthly and material things', 'ascending from base and earthy works and thoughts', 'hidden from the tumult of passions' and the like) are parallel to Evagrius' description of the ascetic life.

[45] Here, the word used, *theoria*, is simply a transliteration from the conventional Greek synonym for *contemplatio*; to distinguish one from the other, I translate *contemplatio* as 'contemplation' and leave *theoria* untranslated.

[46] The simile of the haven was already quite ancient by Cassian's time; see Campbell Bonner, 'Desired Haven', *Harvard Theological Review* 34 (1941), 49-67.

[47] The word translated here as 'asceticism' is *studium*; on this sense of *studium* in Latin ascetic literature, see L. Th. A. Lorié, *Spiritual Terminology in the Latin Translations of the Vita Antonii* (Nijmegen, 1955) 69-74, 78-80, 98-101.

[48] *Akedia* is another Greek ascetic term that Cassian uses without translating it into Latin. For an excellent and evocative description of it, see Evagrius' description of 'the noon-day demon' at *Praktikos* 12 (SC 17 1.520-26). For an excellent discussion of this theme, see G. Bunge, *Akedia. Die geistliche Lehre des Evagrios Pontikos vom Überdruss*, 4th edition (Würzburg: Der Christliche Osten, 1995).

[49] On the 'canonical rule' for using the Psalter in communal prayer, see especially Cassian, *Institutes* 2.

[50] Cassian provides a frank discussion of nocturnal emissions of semen, and how monks coped (or didn't cope) with them, in *Conference* 12.

[51] Columba Stewart has pointed to the ease with which Cassian endorses 'transport of mind' (which he understands as a kind of ecstasy) as an element that sets Cassian apart from Evagrius, to whom he otherwise bears close comparison (as we have seen); see *Cassian the Monk*, 31, 84-86, 105, 108, 113-30. There is no denying that Cassian regularly talks about 'sensation' and uses emotive language with far greater regularity than does Evagrius, but it must not escape our notice that, in the passage, Isaac combines stability of thoughts with keenness of heart and transport of mind. So, whatever else 'transport of mind' might be, it does not jeopardise the stability of one's thoughts and therefore we will want to be very cautious in using the word 'ecstasy' to describe Isaac's teaching.

[52] The word translated 'emotional responses' here and in the following section is *affectus*, which indicates a deep emotional response. Isaac's teaching is that one should learn off by heart the psalter and thus stock oneself with a ready supply of appropriate 'reactions'. This instruction is parallel to the use of scripture promoted by Evagrius Ponticus, especially in his *Refutations* (also known by the Greek title, *Antirrhetikos*), on which, see G. Bunge, 'Evagrios Pontikos: Der Prolog des "Antirrhetikos",' *Studia Monastica* 39 (1997), 77-105.

[53] Cf. *Conference* 9.25, above.

[54] Cf. Mark the Monk, *Concerning those who imagine they are justified by their works* 122: 'Recollection of God is the pain that a person suffers in his heart for the sake of godliness but everyone who forgets God becomes self-indulgent and unfeeling.' This translation is taken from *St Mark the Monk: On the Spiritual Life,* vol. 1, translated by T. Vivian and A. Casiday (Crestwood: SVS Press, 2009).

[55] This line is a paraphrase of Evagrius' *Praktikos* 15 (SC 171: 536): 'Reading and vigils and prayer stabilise the wandering mind...'